THE PURSUIT OF HOLINESS.

Works by the same Author.

An Introduction to the Devotional Study of the Holy Scriptures.

By Edward Meyrick Goulburn. First American from the seventh London edition. 1 vol., 12mo. Cloth, $1.00.

Thoughts on Personal Religion;

Being a Treatise on the Christian Life in its two chief elements, Devotion and Practice. With two new chapters not in previous editions. By Edward Meyrick Goulburn, D. D. With a Prefatory Note by George H. Houghton, D. D. 1 vol., 12mo. Cloth, $1.00.

The Idle Word;

Short Religious Essays on the gift of Speech, and its Employment in Conversation. 1 vol., 12mo. Cloth, $1.00.

Office of the Holy Communion in the Book of Common Prayer.

A Series of Lectures delivered in the Church of St. John the Evangelist. By Edward Meyrick Goulburn. Adapted by the author for the Episcopal Service in the United States. 1 vol., 12mo. Cloth, $1.00.

Sermons Preached on Various Occasions

During the last Twenty Years. By Edward Meyrick Goulburn. 1 vol., 12mo. Cloth, $1.00.

D. APPLETON & CO., Publishers.

THE PURSUIT OF HOLINESS:

A SEQUEL TO

"THOUGHTS ON PERSONAL RELIGION."

INTENDED

TO CARRY THE READER SOMEWHAT FURTHER ONWARD IN THE SPIRITUAL LIFE.

BY

EDWARD MEYRICK GOULBURN, D. D.,

DEAN OF NORWICH,

AND FORMERLY ONE OF HER MAJESTY'S CHAPLAINS IN ORDINARY.

NEW YORK:

D. APPLETON & COMPANY,

90, 92 & 94 GRAND STREET.

1870.

TO

THE EARL OF DERBY, K.G.,

THE ACCOMPLISHED SCHOLAR,

THE BRILLIANT ORATOR,

THE EMINENT STATESMAN;

WHO HAS THOUGHT IT A TASK NOT UNWORTHY

OF HIS GENIUS

TO INSTRUCT YOUNG CHILDREN

IN THE PARABLES OF THE DIVINE WISDOM;

AND TO WHOM THEREFORE

A PLAIN WORK

OF PRACTICAL "INSTRUCTION IN RIGHTEOUSNESS"

MAY BE NOT INAPPROPRIATELY DEDICATED;

THESE PAGES ARE,

BY HIS KIND PERMISSION,

INSCRIBED WITH THE UTMOST RESPECT AND GRATITUDE.

TO THE READER.

A FEW prefatory words on the object of this little treatise, and on the spirit and method in which it is meant to be perused, may, it is hoped, enable the Reader to profit more by it than he otherwise would do, while at the same time it may serve to avert certain criticisms, to which the writer cannot but feel that, as a piece of religious literature, his work is justly exposed.

My "Thoughts on Personal Religion" have met with some success (more, I imagine, because so many are nowadays craving for help and guidance in the matter of personal religion, than on account of any merit or originality in the "Thoughts"); and I have received assurances from trustworthy quarters that the book has been made useful (under God's blessing) to many. Between such persons and myself I feel that a sort of bond has been established, to the obligations of which I desire to be faithful. Our paths in life may never have crossed—nay, we may be very remote from one another (for the book has been kindly and warmly received on the other side of the Atlantic); but they have been pleased to acknowledge themselves as helped by me in the most vitally important of all human concerns; and the acknowledgment has made me almost regard them as if they were my flock, and I their pastor. So I am minded to try to lead them on a little farther, and to rivet the impressions already made upon them, partly by presenting former topics in new lights, partly by guiding them to fields of thought a little less elementary.

It is obvious that this design will lay me open occasionally to the charge of repeating myself. I fully admit such a charge, and am prepared to justify myself under it. Although I have never *consciously* quoted from myself, I doubt not that many passages will be found in this work, bearing a close resemblance (in style as well as sentiment) to others which occur in its predecessor. Must it not of necessity be so in in all books whose scope is to inculcate practical righteousness? Even inspired Apostles were not ashamed of reiterating their exhortations—nay, they regarded their doing so as the security of their disciples: "To write the same things to you, to me indeed is not grievous, but *for you it is safe.*" And St. Peter, in urging upon the faithful that growth in grace, that "going on from strength to strength," whereby alone an "abundant entrance" should "be ministered unto them into the everlasting kingdom of our Lord and Saviour Jesus Christ," expressly says that they needed continual reminding of the necessity of this progress and growth: "Wherefore *I will not be negligent to put you always in remembrance of these things;* though ye know them, and be established in the present truth. Yea, I think it meet, as long as I am in this tabernacle, to stir you up, *by putting you in remembrance.*" Within certain limits nothing new *can* be said (or ought to be demanded) in religious exhortations. All that can be done here in the matter of originality is, that the old truth should be presented in a new light, and (which is of even more importance than newness of aspect) pressed home upon the conscience of the learner with a fresh interest in the mind, and a fresh glow in the heart, of the teacher.

Nor can I think that those readers for whom chiefly this volume is designed, will resent its occasionally speaking in accents with which they are more or less familiar. A man who reads for devotion is not apt to be scandalized by having old truths pressed upon him. It is he only who reads for curiosity, or to amuse his mind with speculative questions, who is impatient of what he has heard before. And this work is designed not so much as a theological treatise (for the composition of which its writer is by no means furnished, and in which character, therefore, it might be found grievously defective) as to be a help to earnest strivers in the spiritual life. It is true that, in parts of it, I have found myself led into an analysis of human motives, and an investigation of human nature, which might seem at first sight to belong rather to the theory than the practice of religion; but this is because I perceive such analysis and investigation really necessary to the satisfactory adjustment of some practical question which has arisen, not because I have for a moment forgotten that I am engaged in endeavoring to direct souls, and to bring myself and others to an experimental knowledge of God. And let me ask you, Reader, in this connection, to regard the book as a book of devotion, and to read it in a method accordant with that view of it. It is offered to you simply as a help in the spiritual life; accept it as such. Do with it as you have done with the many better books of the same character, which from time to time have fallen into your hands. Read it in order, a little at a time, and exercise your mind upon the argument, that you may imbibe whatever may be sound and spiritual in it, and reject whatsoever may be not in accordance with Holy Scripture and the mind of the Universal Church.

And oh! dear soul, created in God's Image, and ransomed with His Blood, whom it has been my desire to serve and help by these instructions, if they shall at any times approve themselves to thee as serviceable and helpful, forget not in thy prayers him who needs such service and help even more than thyself. The authors of such books are almost sure to be thought by strangers far better men than in truth they are. But a moment's consideration of the way in which all works of spiritual counsel must be framed would dissipate the delusion, as well as (it is earnestly hoped) justify the writers from the charge of hypocrisy. Such counsels are addressed, then, in the first instance, to the writer's own heart, on the assumption that his experience will be that of hundreds of others. They are virtually an attack upon his own faults, an exposure of his own weak points, a development of any thought in which he has himself found light, comfort, and encouragement. So far, therefore, from assuming that the writer is himself strong on the points on which he writes strongly, it should rather be assumed that these are the points on which he is really weak,[1] while his conscience and his knowledge of the truth tell him that he ought to be strong. To no higher standard of goodness does such a writer lay claim than this—that he himself strives to live up to the arduous requirements of Christianity; that he is painfully sensible of falling short of the mark; that, like Gideon's troop, he is

[1] To show that I mean what I am saying, I may observe that chap. xv. is directed against a faulty habit of mind, of which I myself am only too conscious.

often "faint," and "yet pursuing;" and that, in the exercise of Christian sympathy, as well as from the desire of making full proof of his ministry, he longs to help those who are experiencing the same difficulties with himself, and to whisper into their ears (whether from the pulpit or the press) any words of light and comfort which may have reached his own soul from above. Without this low degree of Christian experience, no one could hope to make a successful appeal to the hearts and consciences of his fellow-men; and whatever his counsels may seem to import as to his own state, the present writer entreats the reader to give him credit for nothing more. For awful, indeed, are the responsibilities of making a high religious profession; and he who by such a profession lifts himself above the crowd, resembles Nelson, when appearing with all his orders at Trafalgar —he is only too likely to make himself a mark for the fiery darts of the great enemy. How shall we not tremble for the risks which are run by ordinary teachers of Divine truth, when even St. Paul (after and notwithstanding all the sacrifices he had made for Christ) felt that without self-control and mortification of the lower instincts he himself might "become a castaway?" Reader, pray that such may not be the doom of him who in these pages addresses you.

E. M. G.

KISSINGEN, *August* 19, 1869.

CONTENTS.

CHAPTER I.

THAT HOLINESS IS ATTAINABLE.

"*Elias was a man subject to like passions as we are.*"—JAMES v. 17.
"*Of whom the world was not worthy.*"—HEB. xi. 38.

CHAPTER II.

WHAT HAVE WE TO BEGIN UPON?

"*And he would fain have filled his belly with the husks that the swine did eat: and no man gave unto him.*

"*And when he came to himself, he said, How many hired servants of my father's have bread enough and to spare, and I perish with hunger!*

"*I will arise and go to my father.*"—LUKE xv. 16–18.

CHAPTER III.

THE FIRST PRINCIPLE OF HOLINESS, AND HOW TO ATTAIN IT.

"*He entered into the synagogue and taught: and there was a man whose right hand was withered. . . . . . . And looking round about upon them all, He said unto the man, Stretch forth thy*

CHAPTER VI.

THE END OF THE COMMANDMENT, AND THE IMPORTANCE OF KEEPING IT IN VIEW.

"*Now the end of the commandment is charity out of a pure heart, and of a good conscience, and of faith unfeigned: from which some having swerved, have turned aside unto vain jangling.*"—1 TIM. i. 5, 6.

CHAPTER VII.

OF THE VARIOUS SENTIMENTS EMBRACED IN THE LOVE OF GOD.

"*Thou shalt love the Lord thy God with all thy heart, and with all thy soul, and with all thy strength, and with all thy mind.*"—LUKE x. 27.

CHAPTER IX.

OF THE FILIAL RELATION OF MAN TO GOD, UPON WHICH THE LOVE OF GOD IS FOUNDED.

"*God said, Let us make man in our image, after our likeness.*"—GEN. i. 26.

CHAPTER X.

CHAPTER XI.

CHAPTER XIII.

OF PURITY OF MOTIVE.

"*The light of the body is the eye: if therefore thine eye be single, thy whole body shall be full of light. But if thine eye be evil, thy whole body shall be full of darkness. If therefore the light that is in thee be darkness, how great is that darkness!*"—MATT. vi. 22, 23.

CHAPTER XIV.

PEACE OF CONSCIENCE AND OF HEART THE ELEMENT OF HOLINESS.

"*Now the Lord of peace Himself give you peace always by all means.*"—2 THESS. iii. 16.

CHAPTER XV.

PEACE BY LIVING IN THE PRESENT RATHER THAN IN THE PAST.

"*And He said unto another, Follow Me. But he said, Lord, suffer me first to go and bury my father. Jesus said unto him, Let the dead bury their dead: but go thou and preach the kingdom of God.*"—LUKE ix. 59, 60.

CHAPTER XVI.

PEACE BY LIVING IN THE PRESENT RATHER THAN IN THE FUTURE.

"*Be content with such things as ye have.*"—HEB. xiii. 5.

CHAPTER XVII.

THE CENTRIPETAL AND CENTRIFUGAL FORCES OF THE SOUL.

Οὐχὶ πάντες εἰσὶ λειτουργικὰ πνεύματα, εἰς διακονίαν ἀποστελλόμενα διὰ τοὺς μέλλοντας κληρονομεῖν σωτηρίαν; "Are they not all ministering spirits, sent forth to minister for them who shall be heirs of salvation?"—HEB. i. 14.

CHAPTER XVIII.

OF THE NECESSITY OF AN OCCUPATION, AND OF THE RIGHT WAY OF PURSUING IT.

"*Because he was of the same craft, he abode with them, and wrought: for by their occupation they were tent-makers.*"—ACTS xviii. 3.

CHAPTER XIX.

SELF-SACRIFICE A TEST OF THE LOVE OF GOD.

"*And when He was gone forth into the way, there came one running, and kneeled to Him, and asked Him, Good Master, what shall I do that I may inherit eternal life? And Jesus said unto him, Why callest thou Me good? there is none good but One, that is, God. Thou knowest the commandments, Do not commit adultery, Do not kill, Do not steal, Do not bear false witness, Defraud not, Honor thy father and mother. And he answered and said unto Him, Master, all these have I observed from my youth. Then Jesus beholding him loved him, and said unto him, One thing thou lackest: go thy way, sell whatsoever thou hast, and give to the poor, and thou shalt have treasure in heaven: and come, take up the cross, and follow Me.*"—Mark x. 17–21.

CHAPTER XX.

LOVE FOR THE BRETHREN A TEST OF OUR LOVE FOR GOD.

"*If a man say, I love God, and hateth his brother, he is a liar: for he that loveth not his brother whom he hath seen, how can he love God whom he hath not seen?*"—1 JOHN iv. 20.

CHAPTER XXI.

THE LOVE OF GOD A PRINCIPLE RATHER THAN A SENTIMENT.

"*If ye love Me, keep My commandments.*"—JOHN xiv. 15.

CHAPTER XXII.

WHAT SHUTS OUT CHRIST FROM OUR HEARTS?

"*There was no room for them in the inn.*"—LUKE ii. 7.

CHAPTER I.

THAT HOLINESS IS ATTAINABLE.

"*Elias was a man subject to like passions as we are.*"—JAMES v. 17.
"*Of whom the world was not worthy.*"—HEB. xi. 38.

IT needed an Apostle to give us this assurance. If any saint ever seemed to rise above the infirmities of human nature, it was the Prophet Elijah. Elijah was a sort of anchorite, or hermit, who dwelt apart from the haunts of men, except when some errand, on which God sent him, drew him for a time into their neighborhood. He lived, as a rule, not by firesides, but in wildernesses and caverns; his costume was uncouth, his diet simple and austere. Then the power which he exerted over the elements clothes him in our eyes with a supernatural character. He shut up the windows of the sky by his prayers, and by his prayers reopened them. And as he could call down the gracious rain, so could he bid the vengeful fire fall from heaven, and consume those who set themselves against him. And at the close of his career, as if to place a still greater gulf between him and ourselves, his lot was not the common lot of all men. "It is appointed unto men once to die;" but Elijah did not die. He was carried up to heaven by a whirlwind, a chariot of fire and horses of fire appearing as his escort. His was throughout a magnificent and superhuman career.

Yet what is given us of Elijah's history amply bears out the Apostle's assertion that he "was a man of like passions as we are." We read of his being weary of life, and requesting for himself that he might die; of his flying, in a sudden access of terror, from the wrath of Jezebel, though he had bravely confronted Ahab; and of his magnifying himself in prayer as being the only remaining witness for God in Israel, when there were seven thousand men who had not bowed the knee, nor given the kiss of homage, to the image of Baal.

But though the Apostle James instances only in Elias, the truth which he announces, like all truths of Holy Scripture, is one of broad and general import. We are apt to form mistaken notions of God's saints. We are apt to think of them as if they were beings of a different order from ourselves, raised above the level of human infirmity. And from this mistaken notion flows great practical mischief. Not to speak of the manifold evils of saint-worship, which may be supposed to have passed away at the Reformation (though the tendency to it is always alive in the human heart), a wrong estimate of saintliness discourages us for the pursuit of it, as seeming to put it entirely out of our reach.

I. It will be profitable to inquire, first, whence this wrong estimate comes.

It comes chiefly, I suppose, of our looking at the saints from a distance—of our considering them as creatures of the past, not mixed up with the affairs and troubles of life. Whatever we look at from a distance is beautified by the perspective. It is so in bodily sight. A country which was dull, tame, or harsh, when it lay immediately around us, borrows soft and mellow tints from the atmosphere as we recede from it; the blue distance conceals its plain features. It is so with the mental retrospect, which we call memory. Memory has a notorious trick of dropping or smoothing over disagreeables. The days of our childhood, which had their rubs, and their tears, and their faults, like all other days, seem to us always beautiful and innocent in virtue of this trick of memory. The same law of the mind operates to throw round the saints a false and an imaginary lustre. We imagine that no man is or can be a saint who is mixed up in the daily intercourse of society, who is fighting hand to hand with us in the battle of life. Why not? What one sound reason can be assigned why there should not be nowadays men as zealous, as devoted, as simple-minded, as the Apostles and saints of the primitive Church? It might perhaps be imagined that Christianity, when it came as a fresh force into human nature, when it presented itself with all the interest of a new revelation, wrought moral wonders which, since the mind of man has become familiar with its truths, it is powerless to work. But this is to suppose that Christianity depends for its success on the ordinary constitution of the human mind, and to overlook the fact that it employs in its service supernatural forces and agencies. "Is the Lord's arm shortened that it cannot save?" Are men's hearts, in the nineteenth century, beyond the reach of His grace? Is the moral paralysis of the Church in these latter days such, that even the Spirit cannot put life into the withered hand? Has the blood of the Lord Jesus lost its cleansing and sanctifying power? Is it not rather true, as the Christian poet sings, that

> "Fresh as when it first was shed
> Springs forth the Saviour's Blood?"

Or was the promise of grace limited to the first believers, and not rather expressly extended "to you and to your children, and to all that are afar off" ("afar off" in every sense of the words, in religious position, in space, in time), "even as many as the Lord our God shall call?"

II. Let us see now how the Scriptures counteract this mistaken notion of sanctity. It has been already pointed out how Elijah is exhibited to us as showing moral weakness in two great features of it—weariness of life, and want of patience. But the saints of the New Testament, in whom we naturally expect to find a higher standard, are also exhibited to us—we cannot doubt with a deep purpose—as exempt neither from infirmity nor error. I will not instance in such points as St. Peter's fall, because this took place before the disciples had been endued with power from on high by the descent of the Holy Spirit on the day of Pentecost; but I take the quarrel between St. Paul and St. Barnabas, as recorded in the fifteenth chapter of the Acts, which led to a dissolution of the partnership between them. How very like it is to those differences among good men nowadays, which so often issue—so much to the Church's loss—in divided operations! On one side is the partiality of natural affection. John Mark, whom St. Barnabas has fixed upon as the companion of the Apostolic tour, was the sister's son of that

Apostle, who was ready therefore to condone his nephew's past misconduct. On the other side, Paul, with his burning zeal, had been justly offended by the half-heartedness of John Mark, when he had accompanied them on their previous journey. Disliking, no doubt, the inconveniences and hardships to which their companionship subjected him, Mark had "departed from them from Pamphylia, and went not with them to the work." St. Paul took strongly the view that this conduct was a disqualification for a second trial of the young man. Had not the Lord Jesus Himself said, "No man, having put his hand to the plough, and looking back, is fit for the kingdom of God?" Doubtless St. Paul was not wholly and utterly in the right. He would have been cooler in the dispute that followed had he been so. Doubtless, he was for showing too little indulgence to one who, though he had been overtaken in a fault, yet now, by his willingness to accompany them on their second voyage, showed himself sensible of it. In short, St. Paul hardly acted in this case on his own inspired counsel to "restore such an one in the spirit of meekness." So the collision of natural affection in Barnabas with the somewhat unchastened, untempered zeal of Paul produced a sharp contention—in the original it is "a paroxysm"—between them. Sharp words passed, and mutual recriminations, and the feelings of both parties were exasperated—alas! so much so, that they found it impossible to work together; they must henceforth choose different spheres of duty. How! Are these Apostles? Are these two of God's most eminent saints? Are these two eminent pillars of the Church of Christ? Yes, reader;

Apostles, and saints, and pillars, not as our fancy portrays them, nor as they are now, in the calm and deep repose of Paradise, but as they were in the struggles and collisions of daily life—"men of like passions as we are"—not always subduing those passions, and only subduing them at all by that grace which is offered to us as freely as to them.

But let us now fasten our thoughts on another point in the history of the New Testament Saints, which often seems to be strangely overlooked. We are apt to form most erroneous notions of what the descent of the Holy Ghost did for the Disciples of Christ. We are apt to think that it endued them in an instant of time with fulness of knowledge, and fulness of sanctity—that it dispelled from their mind all prejudice and error, and raised the curtain at once upon the full panorama of Divine Truth. But what are the facts of history? The facts are that eight years after the descent of the Holy Spirit, it required a vision, and a providential indication, and withal a direct injunction of the Holy Ghost, to induce St. Peter to accept and act upon the truth, that the Gentiles were to be no more regarded as strangers and foreigners, but to become fellow-citizens with the saints and of the household of God. And though these circumstances must have impressed the truth of the Gentiles' fellow-heirship ineffaceably upon his heart and mind, we find him afterward guilty of moral cowardice in hiding his convictions on the subject. Though now of some standing in the Apostleship, and confirmed (one would think) in his views of Christian Truth, he appears to have forgotten his Master's warnings against putting the light under a bushel, and not allowing it to shine before men.

"When Peter was come to Antioch," says St. Paul, "I withstood him to the face, because he was to be blamed. For before that certain came from James, he did eat with the Gentiles: but when they were come, he withdrew, and separated himself, fearing them which were of the circumcision. And the other Jews dissembled likewise with him; insomuch that Barnabas also was carried away with their dissimulation." And who is this, who (if the Word of God be true) thus exhibited narrowness and moral cowardice on a critical occasion, and drew others away after him into compliance with his mischievous example? This is the Rockman,[1] on whom the Lord said that He would build His Church, and to whom He solemnly intrusted the keys of the Kingdom of Heaven; this is a saint specially dear to Christ, and specially honored of Him; a saint who was enabled to perform many mighty and wonderful works, and whose very shadow was healing, an emblem this of the wholesome spiritual influences which the holy life and conversation of St. Peter diffused around him. Verily "Elias was a man subject to like passions as we are."

The truth is (and it is a truth most apposite to the whole argument of the present work) that the Holy Spirit, as given to the Church, and to each member of

[1] I call him "Rockman," as the most suitable word I can coin to express the etymology of the name which Our Lord gave him (Πέτρος = Πέτρα-ος = Rock, with a masculine termination). An able note on the interpretation of Matt. xvi. 18, 19, repudiating both errors—that of the Papists, which regards St. Peter as the rock, *independently of his confession*, and that of the Protestants, which regards the confession (and not the Apostle) as the rock, will be found in "Schaff's History of the Apostolic Church" (Edinburgh: T. & T. Clark, 1854), vol. ii., pp. 5, 6.

the Church, is not an illumination once for all, or a confirmation once for all, but a germ of light and strength capable of indefinite development. It is potentially, *but only potentially*, a revelation of all truth to the intellect, and a communication of all power to the will. It is a growing and expansive force, not a force which exhausts itself in one impulse. In short, it is a seed, not a full-formed flower; and, like all seeds, its growth is liable to checks and drawbacks. It is planted in the poor, barren soil of the human heart, which by nature engenders weeds only. It shoots up into the climate of a wicked world. And just as, in the world of nature, plants are exposed to blight, which is said to be composed of hosts of minute insects, so in the moral world Grace is apt to be thwarted by the legions of fallen angels, whom the Scriptures speak of as swarming around us on every side, "principalities and powers, and the rulers of the darkness of this world." What wonder if the spiritual development of saints be often thrown back, and if their best graces be sadly marred by infirmities?

III. We have been endeavoring to correct the popular notion of saints as men exempt from our infirmities and altogether exalted above our sphere. But this notion has another tendency, besides that which has been already discussed. It leads not only to what we may call an overvaluation of those saints who have long since passed away, but to an undervaluation of those who may now be (if we had eyes to see them) fighting the battle of life by our side. And against this error also the Word of God protests, teaching us, in another passage, that "the world is not worthy" of God's saints.

Every man and woman who lives by Christian principle (that is, by faith), who sustains the life of his immortal spirit by prayer, and sacraments, and the Word of God, and resists evil watchfully and steadfastly, IS a saint. He may have his infirmities, his backslidings, his periods of lukewarmness, his failings of temper, his moral cowardice; so had the Scriptural saints. And our close commerce with him in life, forcing upon us, as it does, his weaknesses and prejudices, while his communion with God, transacted in the depths of his own spirit, is of course screened from us, hinders, for the present, our fully appreciating him. We see very clearly that he is "a man subject to like passions as we are;" but we fail to see that he is Elijah. Perchance we shall see this too by-and-by, when he is taken from us. Sanctity in our friends and neighbors is like a star. We take no notice of the star while the sun is pouring his rays over the firmament, and the full stir of life is around us. But let the night draw her curtain over the sky; and the star in all its beauty steals out to view. So while our friends are mixed up with us in the hurry and commerce of life, we seem unable to disentangle from their infirmities the saintliness which is in them. But they die; and something comes to light about their inward life which hitherto had escaped every eye but God's, and we begin to discover that the commonest things they did were governed by Christian principle, and referred to God in prayer, and perhaps that we have been for years walking side by side with angels unawares. Death has now thrown his pall over them; they are no longer in the hubbub of life or the strife of tongues; and the star of their sanctity begins to twinkle brightly to our eyes. Oh! lest remorse for having appreciated God's saints so little should strike a chill to our hearts, when they are taken from us, let us now be on the watch for any tokens of good in one another, and hail such tokens with affectionate reverence. Let not infirmities, however patent, blind our eyes to the grace which there may be in a brother. Let us hope for good in him, promptly believe in it, joyfully welcome it. And let us not fail to bless God for every example of faith and love given by His people, whether still in a state of warfare, or departed to their rest, "beseeching Him to give us grace so to follow their good examples, that with them we may be partakers of His heavenly kingdom."

To revert again, in conclusion, to the great lesson of this Chapter. The greatest saints who ever lived, whether under the Old or New Dispensations, are on a level which is quite within our reach. The same forces of the spiritual world which were at their command, and the exertion of which made them such spiritual heroes, are open to us also. If we had the same faith, the same hope, the same love which they exhibited, we could achieve marvels as great as those which they achieved—not indeed in marvels which change the outward face of Nature, but those higher marvels, whose field is the heart and soul of man. A word of prayer in our mouths would be as potent to call down the gracious dews and the melting fires of God's Spirit, as it was in Elijah's mouth to call down literal rain and fire, if we could only speak the word with that full assurance of faith wherewith he said it. Let us no more say querulously, as an excuse to our consciences for not prosecuting the high end to which we are called, "God has put the great standards of holiness out of my reach." IT IS NOT SO. As if with the design of meeting such an objection, He exhibits to us in His Word the occasional failures and feebleness of His most illustrious servants, and gives us a glimpse of them, not only in the triumphs of Grace, but in the infirmities of Nature. Seen in plain truth, and not through the distorting medium of distance, they were "men of like passions with ourselves," though under the empire of principles which brought God into immediate relation with them, and thus lifted them above self and the world. Why should we not follow them, even as they followed God and Christ? Plainly the reason is not to be sought in any disadvantages under which we labor, in comparison of them. It is not that holiness was originally more congenial to their nature than to ours. It is not that privileges accorded to them are denied to us. It can be nothing but that laggardness of will, that indifference to high moral aims, that want of spiritual energy, that cheerful acquiescence in the popular standard of religion, which has caused many a soul, when "weighed in the balances," to be "found wanting," to be counted unworthy of the calling and the Kingdom of God.

CHAPTER II.

WHAT HAVE WE TO BEGIN UPON?

"*And he would fain have filled his belly with the husks that the swine did eat: and no man gave unto him.*

"*And when he came to himself, he said, How many hired servants of my father's have bread enough and to spare, and I perish with hunger!*

"*I will arise and go to my father.*"—LUKE xv. 16–18.

THE scope of our observations in the last Chapter was to show that saintliness is not something unattainable, or beyond our reach, inasmuch as the most eminent saints, both of the Old and New Testaments, are clearly proved to have been "men of like passions as we are." The next question will be, How are we to proceed in attaining it? and, first, How are we to begin? The answer to this first question is specially important. For the principles which must guide us in the prosecution of this great work are the very same which must guide us at its commencement. So that the beginning is not a beginning merely, but a beginning which has a development wrapped up in it; it is a seed which has only to burst and shoot up, in order to become a blade, and then consecutively an ear, and the full corn in the ear. "As ye have therefore received Christ Jesus the Lord, so walk ye in

Him," says the Apostle to the Colossians, showing clearly that Christian progress proceeds in the very same method as the commencement of Christian life. And therefore in this work, more, perhaps, than in any other, it is true (and the thought is most encouraging to those who are disposed to begin), that "Dimidium facti qui cœpit habet," "he who has begun has advanced half-way toward the end."

Upon what are we to begin, then, if we desire to follow after Holiness? I answer, upon the grace of our Baptism: this is the grand starting-point of all Christian effort. And the special blessing of *Infant* Baptism is this, that God in it "prevents" us (in the old sense of the word "prevents"), anticipates us with His Grace, anticipates consciousness, anticipates temptation, anticipates sin, so that, when the powers of evil throw up their approaches to the soul, they find the Holy Spirit in possession of the fortress before them. And thus, before one who is baptized in infancy can be soiled by evil, he is tinctured with good.

In order to the development of this thought, it will be necessary to say something of the relationship which is contracted by Baptism, and next of the grace which is bestowed in it.

I. First, the relationship contracted by Baptism. "Baptism, wherein I was made a child of God." There is a strange confusion of thought on the subject of this relationship, a confusion which has the mischievous result of dividing good men, who, were it not for this, would all "speak the same thing." By Baptism a relationship with God is contracted, the baptized person being admitted into His family. It is strange that persons cannot see that a relationship stands clear altogether of the moral conduct of the person holding it, and cannot be in any way affected or shaken by that moral conduct. The prodigal son in the Parable was a son still, all his profligate and ungrateful conduct notwithstanding. His leaving the home of his childhood, his taking up his abode in a far country, his squandering his fortune, his connection with vile, outlandish women, his abject poverty, his ultimate degradation to the office of swineherd, all these things did not alter his lineage, nor drain his father's blood out of his veins. He said, and he felt, that *he was not worthy* to be called a son; but in the same breath he called his father "Father," showing that the relationship was not annihilated, however unworthy of it he had proved. It is so with God's children, who are adopted into His family by Baptism. Nothing which occurs in after-life can raze the seal off the bond of their Baptism. However they may dishonor and cast a stain upon their divine lineage, it still exists. And hence it was that Luther called upon sinners, as the first effort in the direction of Repentance, to go back to their Baptism, and to stand upon that before God. He felt that the baptismal relationship must be for a christened man the very ground and foundation of all his subsequent dealings with God.

There are, it is true, passages of Holy Scripture (let us not blink one of them) which seem expressly to connect Divine Sonship with abstinence from sin and correspondence to grace, and which at first sight forbid us to predicate that sonship where these features of character do not exist. The strongest passages of this sort I can think of are, "As many as are *led* by the Spirit of God, they are the sons of God;" and, "Whosoever is born of God doth not commit sin; for His seed remaineth in him, and he cannot sin, because he is born of God." But these and the like words are capable of an easy explanation, which renders them consistent not only with the doctrine of baptismal Regeneration, but also with the analogy of natural sonship. Might not a father say of a very vile son, who had brought a stain upon the honor of his family, "He is no son of mine; I can trace in him nothing of my character and disposition; I disown him altogether, and recognize only those of my children who maintain the credit of my name?" In saying this, no one would understand him to deny the natural relationship of the bad son to him, but only to repudiate in the strongest terms he could find any *moral* affinity. In God's family too there is a sonship of moral affinity, as well as a far wider sonship of Sacramental relation, and of course it is only those who exhibit the sonship of moral affinity who will be recognized as sons at the Great Day; all else will be repudiated and solemnly disowned by our Heavenly Father.

II. Having thus explained the baptismal relationship, we will now point out the grace which it carries along with it, and which may be defined as the first force — the earliest motive-power — of the Christian life. Did I say I would point it out? But it lies under our hands, though, like other things which lie under our hands, we are apt to miss it, because we search for it too far afield. The shape which the baptismal grace takes in all men in general is good desires. You have these good desires attributed to grace, and to "special grace" in the Easter Collect:—"As, by Thy special grace preventing us, Thou dost put into our minds *good desires.*" Our esteem for devout and religious people, the wish to be good and to lead a devout and religious life, the wish to amend and shake off bad habits, and conquer faults of character—these at the lower end of the scale; and at the higher, the restlessness and emptiness engendered in the heart by a day without prayer, the calm which earnest prayer is felt to induce, and the desire after prayer which results from these experiences; the longing, too, after Holy Communion combined, as it often is, with a fear of approaching the ordinance unworthily—these are some of the impulses, more or less fluctuating, more or less allowed to color the life, more or less strong, according to the occasions which call them forth and the characters of the persons harboring them, which spring up continually in the heart of the baptized, and which represent the action of the Holy Spirit upon the soul, in virtue of Baptism.[1] *They are not the fruit which God*

[1] It will no doubt be said that persons merely educated in Christian Truth, and submitted freely to the influences of Christian civilization—children, for instance, of a Baptist or a Quaker—would probably have all the sentiments here described, even without the administration of the Sacrament of Baptism. No doubt Christian education, which Our Lord ordained *in close and vital connection with the Sacrament of Baptism* ("*baptizing* them in the name of the Father, and of the Son, and of the Holy Ghost; *teaching* them to observe all things whatsoever I have commanded you," Matt. xxviii. 19, 20), has of itself a great effect in instilling

will require in its season from those who have been planted in His vineyard; but they are the blossom on the fruit-tree, an efflorescence, which shows the tree's vitality, and gives hope that, with proper culture, it will bear fruit hereafter.

But in those who have fallen into wilful and deliberate sin, and, it may be, have long persisted in that evil course, the grace of Baptism, unless, indeed, it has become altogether extinct, operates in another manner. The parable of the Prodigal Son beautifully illustrates this working of the grace in question. The son had tried to live on unsatisfying food, and had found by experience that it could not fill or nourish him. The craving of natural appetite brought him to himself, and it was then that he began to bethink him of the abundant diet provided even for menials in his father's house: "How many hired servants of my father's have bread enough and to spare, and I perish with hunger!" It is very observable that his earliest instigation to return arises from nothing nobler than a sense that he was famishing. It is not, in the first instance, love for his father; it is not a touching memory of earlier and purer days sweeping across his heart, which moves him to retrace his steps; but merely the gnawing of hunger. Oh, great and gra-

these "good desires." But the fact that God is good and gracious, even to those who have never formally been brought into the bond of His Covenant, and is pleased sometimes to attach grace to that which is only half a Sacrament, cannot disprove the normal connection between Baptism and those drawings of the heart which are here said to be its effects. The warmth of incubation is the usual and regular means of quickening the germ of life in an egg: that chickens may be hatched by artificial warmth does not really make against this truth.

cious encouragement to a sinner who has wandered far from God, and seems quite to have estranged himself from his heavenly home! The mere dissatisfaction with the creature, arising from making trial of it and finding it to fail, the mere void which is created in the heart by constant disappointment, when all worldly sources of happiness have been proved one after another, and turned out broken cisterns which can hold no water—even this motive, interested and selfish as it is, is accepted, if it lead to an effective penitence, or rather to a hearty effort in that direction. And why? Because this intense dissatisfaction of the soul with the creature, this refusal to acquiesce in any thing which does not fully content the heart, is instigated by the Holy Spirit, is an impulse of baptismal grace, still struggling with the reluctant will. It may be grace in its earliest stage, but grace it is, inasmuch as it leads the heart of man to realize a great truth which it is naturally averse to accept,—the truth of the creature's emptiness. And God cannot turn His back on His own grace, when He sees one of His children led by it, and yielding to its impulse.

I said it was not *primarily* love for his father, nor memory of his home, which instigated the prodigal's return. But we cannot exclude these feelings from a share in determining his conduct. Scarcely ever do men, and least of all penitents, act from pure and unmixed motives. What sentiment, then, do we find kneaded up with that emptiness and sense of want which appears to have been his primary motive? The sentiment finds an utterance in that word "Father." He had been very hard for a long time as regarded home ties; but the old affection was not quite dead, it still smouldered under the cinders of youthful passions, which now had burned themselves out and formed a charred crust over his heart. And now it reasserted itself very significantly; "I will arise," says he, "and go to my father." I believe that when God is truly and evangelically set forth as the Father of the human spirit, really related to it by a bond of which earthly fatherhood is only a poor, thin, unsubstantial shadow, there is hardly any soul so lost in sin that it will not make a response, and cry out of the depths of its ruin, "Verily, Thou art my Father." St. Philip said a much profounder thing than he meant, when he made that request to his Master, "Lord, show us the Father, and it sufficeth us." That is just the utterance of the human soul under the earlier promptings of grace, when it wakes up to the experience that nothing earthly *does* suffice, and yet feels that there must be somewhere something which corresponds to its boundless cravings after good. Hearing in the Gospel of a Father who is all Wisdom and all Love, as well as boundless in power, the soul recognizes the manifestation of this Father as its one true want. "Show me the Father," it cries, "and it sufficeth me." I borrow from an eminent devotional writer a quaint but beautiful illustration of this truth. He says that there are birds which hatch the eggs of other birds of the same species, and rear a brood which is not their own; but that when a bird thus reared happens to hear the cry of its own real mother, by a marvellous operation of instinct it flies toward her, and takes its place under her wings. "Even so," he says, "our heart, though reared and nourished under the wings of Nature, amidst the material and transitory objects of the earth, yet no sooner hears a true representation of the Heavenly Father, than it feels drawn toward Him by a spiritual instinct, the operation of which shows that it was made for God originally, and that in God only can it find rest."

My dear readers, is there any one of you, however hard and indifferent to true religion he may at present seem to be, who does not feel an interest in these observations? Is there any one of you, however worldly and careless, nay, bad and vicious, he may be, whose stagnant heart is not from time to time stirred by an earnest wish that he were better? Well, even that wish is a pure breath from heaven, wafted to you (as it were) across the waters of your Baptism. Is there any one, however sunk into spiritual insensibility, who does not feel somewhat attracted by the testimony of a Heavenly Father, and in whose heart there does not spring up, on such a testimony being made, an irrepressible desire to know something of this Father? Is there any one, however happy his lot, whose lot altogether contents him, so that he can say, "I have enough?" Then, if these and the like aspirations from time to time find place in your hearts, why do you not follow in the direction in which they lead? Why do you not cast off sin, or make such a resolute effort to cast it off, and take such a stride in that direction as God may meet half-way? Remember, that the penitent son had not completed his return—he was yet "a great way off" from his home—had only his face set and his steps bent homeward, when "his father saw him, and had compassion, and ran, and fell on his neck, and kissed him." If the thought of God is so attractive, why not suffer yourself to be drawn by it? Why not seek God in prayer, through the name of His Son? Is He so overabundantly "loving unto every man," and will He be able to restrain His bowels of compassion, if He sees a soul struggling toward Him as best it may? Remember, at all events, that you are responsible for the use you make of the good instigations which from time to time visit your heart. They are given you for a purpose, to begin the spiritual life upon, to be the starting-point of holy effort and prayer. You are not the better man for *having* them, for they come of free grace, not of nature; but you *are* the better for surrendering yourself to them, and following their lead. I say following their lead; for what the Holy Spirit does is to lead—and to move, in order that He may lead. Do not imagine that He does more. Do not imagine that he drives or compels. To do so would be to destroy the moral nature of the creature, instead of renewing it. The Holy Spirit extends His hand to us, entices, allures, invites, remonstrates, but never forces. Let us place our hand in His, and make ourselves over to His guidance. The way may be occasionally thorny and rough, but it ends in such a vision of God's perfections as will fully content the soul; yea, it ends in that knowledge of Him, "wherein standeth our eternal life."

CHAPTER III.[1]

THE FIRST PRINCIPLE OF HOLINESS, AND HOW TO ATTAIN IT.

"*He entered into the synagogue and taught: and there was a man whose right hand was withered. . . . . . . And looking round about upon them all, He said unto the man, Stretch forth thy hand, and he did so: and his hand was restored whole as the other.*"—LUKE vi. 6, 10.

IT is probable that many persons are deterred from beginning a religious course in right earnest by a feeling that the very beginning is out of their own reach. Faith, they know, is the great principle of the spiritual life; the just man lives by his faith. But then faith is declared to be the gift of God, not the product of human effort. And therefore their notion is, that faith drops upon people from Heaven quite arbitrarily, according to no known laws, and that there is no regular and prescribed method for the attainment of it. Though surely the mere consideration of God's infinite goodness might teach these people that He cannot possibly lay upon us a command which He

[1] The substance of this Chapter appeared many years ago in a volume of Parochial Sermons, preached by me in my (then) Church of Holywell, in Oxford. But I have rewritten the whole argument for the purpose of the present work.

will not give us power to obey, and that, therefore, since He bids us believe the Gospel, or (in other words) exercise faith in Christ, it must be within our power, aided by His gracious Spirit, to do so.

I believe we shall nowhere better see the true relation between God's gift of faith, and the part which human effort has to play in the attainment of it, than in the narrative of the cure wrought by Our Lord upon a man that had a withered hand.

A withered hand; of what spiritual defect is this bodily defect a type or figure? The hand is the organ of touch. He, therefore, whose hand is withered, has lost the sense of touch in that which is the chief organ of the sense. Now consider what impressions we gain from the sense of touch. It is touch which, more than any other sense, convinces us of the reality of matter. What you see might be merely a phantom, an optical illusion, a picture painted on the retina of the eye, and nothing more; but if you go up to the thing you see, and touch it, and handle it, you become assured of its existence, you know that it is substantial. Now what is faith? It may be defined as the faculty by which we realize unseen things—such as the Being and Presence of God, the work which Our Lord did for us, the future judgment, the future recompense of the righteous, and the like unseen things.

I say the faculty (not by which we conceive, but) by which we realize these things, feel them to have a body and a substance. To imagine the truths of Religion is not to believe them. We may from time to time imagine God as He is in Heaven, surrounded by myriads of glorious angels—we may imagine Christ looking down upon us from God's right hand, interceding for us, calling us to account at the last day, and awarding to us our final doom; but the mere picturing these things to ourselves is not the same thing as believing them; the believing them is the having such a conviction of their reality, as to live under their influence, and to be in some measure at least governed by them. In short, to *imagine* the truths of religion is like surveying things by the eye; to *believe* in the truths of religion is like grasping the same things with the hand, and thus proving them to have substance and consistency. I need say no more to show that a withered hand, being a hand without the sense of touch, is a very just and suitable emblem of the soul of the natural man, which has lost the power of faith. For faith is nothing more nor less than *the faculty of spiritual touch.*

The patient, however, on whose story we are founding these remarks, had not lost the sense of touch altogether. It was only his right hand which was withered; he could handle things with his left. And this may usefully remind us of what has often been pointed out, that man by nature is not a stranger to faith or to its power—that he *does* exercise it, though within a very limited horizon. Yes, surely. Every victory which man has achieved over Nature has been achieved in the power of faith. The husbandman ploughs and sows in full persuasion of a harvest—that persuasion is faith. The man in full health and full work lays by a part of his earnings against a time when he shall be able to work no longer: that act of saving is an act of faith; for why does he save but that he believes a time of decrepitude and infirmity will surely come to him, though at present there are no symptoms of it? All the many precautions, which we take against evil contingencies—precautions which follow everywhere in the train of civilization—are all instances of faith, and of its power in man's natural life. For the future, against which these precautions are taken, is unseen, and faith is the only faculty which grasps the unseen, which brings it home to us, and gives it a living power. The strange and melancholy thing is, that our faith has no power of grasping such things as lie beyond the horizon of time and experience. Ask it to realize judgment to come, or a future state of existence, or the Presence of God, or the intercession of Christ, or any of the unseen things of which with no uncertain voice the Word of God assures us,—and it drops paralyzed by our sides: the hand—the right or better hand, that which might enable us, if it retained the sense of touch, to realize things nobler than any which enter into human experience—is withered.

Now let us learn from the narrative the method of restoration. It is plain, in the first place, that the restorative power was in Christ, and dependent absolutely and entirely upon His will. When Our Lord willed it—neither sooner nor later—the healing virtue with which His Sacred Person was charged flew into the withered hand, and made it in an instant of time whole as the other. The patient's will, the patient's effort, could have done nothing whatever for him, independently of Christ. No exercise, prescribed to him by human skill, could have done aught to help him, had not the gracious Source of all health, natural and spiritual, been present as a fountain from which he might draw. I say, a fountain from which he might draw; for you observe, in the second place, that, being in the presence of the fountain, *he was required to draw.* Our Lord did not by a mere act of His own will restore his hand—He bade the man to do something. And what He bade him to do sounded impossible in the present circumstances of the patient. He told him to stretch forth his hand,—a hand which was probably cramped together and curved by the complaint,—a hand in which there was no muscular power, and over which the brain had no control. And yet there was a meaning in the command, and a meaning which the patient understood. The meaning was that he should try to act as if the withered hand had been sound,—try to unclinch those fast-set fingers, to unroll that long-closed palm. Very probably the thought flashed like lightning across the poor creature's mind: "He has healed hundreds who simply did as He bade them. He bids me to do this; and therefore I must be equal to doing this, or at least He will make me equal." "And he stretched it forth,"—he made the effort which he had been bidden to make,—his will roused itself,—his brain issued once more the order which hitherto, as regarded that member, had produced no effect; and he finds with delight that the order is now obeyed, the hand unrolls itself, stretches itself toward the Saviour, casts off its old incapacity, is restored whole as the other.

One more observation we will draw from the narrative, before we part company with it. A hand stretched forth toward Christ is the emblem of prayer. Now as faith is the one great *principle* of the Spiritual Life, so is prayer its one great *exercise.* And though prayer is a very simple thing, and it is perfectly easy to grasp the idea of going to God for what we want, and telling out before Him the desires of our hearts; all experience teaches that prayer—at all events, stated and continuous prayer—is very difficult to practise. Those who are not much in the habit of collecting their thoughts, and are brought for the first time to see the necessity of real earnest prayer proceeding from the heart's core, find that the distractions which beset every attempt so to pray are "Legion;" the mind is always flying off at a tangent to the concerns or amusements of this life; it seems to be the sport of every trifling impulse; teased and rebuffed, it finds its half-hour of devotion turned into a half-hour of bitter mortification. And even the best Christians, and those who have made some progress in the discipline of the mind, ever and anon find their prayers a grievous disappointment; they had looked to find a comfort and a sedative in prayer, looked that it might lift them a little out of the atmosphere of this world; but they are crossed, and checked, and thwarted at every turn, being made in this way practically to feel their dependence upon God for the Spirit of grace and supplications. In this condition of mind it is natural to turn away from the faldstool in disgust, and postpone devotion to a more convenient season. We are apt to say peevishly, "I cannot pray just now; I will put it off till circumstances are more favorable, till the mind is less anxious and less volatile, till the animal spirits flow more readily." Ah! this is not the true policy. The true policy is to persist in spite of the annoyances and the rebuffs. The true policy in spiritual things *always* is to endeavor, and to go on endeavoring, after that which we feel quite unequal to do.

The motto of this policy is, " Stretch forth thy hand;" if the needful help does not seem to come immediately, it will come as soon as God sees that your faith and patience are sufficiently approved. Where you cannot pray as you wish, pray at all events as you can; do not allow yourself to be teased away from your post of duty; make a more vigorous endeavor. Great was the reward which people of old carried away, who, like the Syrophœnician woman, or the bearers of the paralytic patient, hung on to the Lord in spite of discouragement, and would take no denial. Remember that no principle is shown by praying when the course of prayer runs smooth, when the mind is in order and composed, and the exercise acts as a sedative to the soul. To glide into harbor in a smooth sea, and with wind and tide both favoring, is no trial of a vessel at all. But to persist in making for the harbor with an adverse wind and tide, courageously to tack and tack again in hopes of making a little headway, and coming a little nearer to the mark, and so to wait on, striving against all odds, till wind and tide come round —this tries both the ribs of the ship and the patience of the mariners. And God must surely find that prayer most acceptable, in which He sees the greatest trial of principle.

We have now arrived at the point at which we can see distinctly how a beginning of the Christian life may be made by any one who is willing to make it. In our last chapter we spoke of the grace which accompanies the baptismal relationship, and which exhibits itself in " good desires," those relentings as to a sinful or a thoughtless and careless career, those dissatisfactions with the world and with self, those attractions of the mind toward God, when scripturally exhibited as the Father of the human spirit, which spring up ever and anon in men's hearts—to be summarily suppressed by some, to be cherished and brought to good effect by others. To surrender one's self in earnest to these good desires, to follow whither they lead, is the first thing to be done; and God will not lead us forward, until we have really mastered the first step. We shall not have followed far in the direction of these impulses, before it will begin to dawn upon us that what we really need in order to victory over sin and the world is *a true faith*, a realizing grasp of unseen things, such a grasp as gives a body and a substance to the truths respecting Heaven and Hell, God, and Christ, and the Devil, taking them out of the category of chimeras (or notions) and placing them in that of realities. Well, such a faith is to be had. It may be derived from Christ into our souls, as it has been derived into thousands of souls before ours. But think not that the Lord gives so priceless a blessing to those who do not show themselves worthy of it. Think not that He gives it to listless or languid seekers. Even human knowledge cannot be won without strenuous effort. Pearls cannot be picked up without the risk and trouble of diving for them. Ask of God the restoration of the lost sense of spiritual touch. If you are troubled and rebuffed by distractions in your prayer, pray on; "stretch forth thy hand" at the gate of Mercy, till something is put into it from above. And strive too; or how else shall you yourself be assured of the sincerity of your prayer? Act up to present light. Rouse yourself to shake off every thing in your present course, which an enlightened conscience condemns. Set about amending faults of character and conduct. Act as faith would lead you to act, even when your faith is feeble, or rather seems to you to be none. And the faithful endeavor shall assuredly in God's good time be crowned with success. The virtue that is in Christ shall pass into the withered hand; and then the eternal things, that are not seen, shall have for thee the same reality, and exert upon thee the same influence, as the things that are seen and temporal.

CHAPTER IV.

THE POINT OF DEPARTURE IN THE RIGHT COURSE.

"*For the invisible things of Him from the creation of the world are clearly seen, being understood by the things that are made, even His eternal power and Godhead; so that they are without excuse: because that, when they knew God, they glorified Him not as God, neither were thankful; but became vain in their imaginations, and their foolish heart was darkened. Professing themselves to be wise, they became fools, and changed the image of the uncorruptible God into an image made like to corruptible man, and to birds, and four-footed beasts, and creeping things. Wherefore God also gave them up to uncleanness through the lusts of their own hearts, to dishonor their own bodies between themselves.*"—ROM. i. 20–24.

THE passage which stands at the head of this chapter is a profound piece of Christian philosophy. And from the study of it we may gain a great insight into the secret and source of Holiness, in the pursuit of which we are engaged. It teaches us that large and exalted conceptions of God are the spring of all virtue.

The Apostle is speaking of the deep degradation into which man has fallen by his vices—vices, many of them, which it is a shame to speak of—vices against which Nature herself protests, and to which the lower animals are strangers. In the passage quoted above he gives an account of this degradation—traces it up to its true source. Now observe how different is the Apostle's account of man's degradation from that which a mere moralist gives. The moralist tells us that conscience is a sovereign faculty, bearing upon its brow the stamp of authority, and evidently intended to sway and control the appetites and affections. This faculty, however, has been dethroned; the unruly passions (in themselves mere brute impulses) have usurped its seat, and domineer over the will, which becomes their slave and does their bidding. This, no doubt, is true as far as it goes, but it goes only a very short way. It simply points us to the machinery of our nature as being in a disorganized state, and shows us in what the disorganization consists; but it does not trace up the disorganization to its primary cause.

And yet it is a practical, as well as a curious and interesting question, what may have been the point of starting, from which man ultimately reached that lowest depth of moral degradation, to which he has so often sunk. In the frightful, hideous vices which abound in great cities, we see at once that there is an enormous divergence from the rule of right. But where exactly did the divergence begin? Two lines which parted company at a certain point, are now running on at a distance of many miles from each other in wholly opposite directions; but when first they parted company, there was only a hair's-breadth of space between them. What was the exact point of divergence, at which man parted company from right, and commenced his downward course? Perhaps, as in the case of the lines, the deviation will not seem very serious at the outset, though its ultimate result is so frightful. It is this question which the Apostle answers in the passage before us. Man's moral degradation, he says, is a retribution—and a retribution in kind (pray observe how, in the moralist's account of the matter, the personality of God was altogether left out of the question; whereas in that of the Apostle, God is brought on the stage at once, and the whole degradation is said to be a judicial infliction by Him). Man had degraded God, says the Apostle, and God degraded man. But how had man degraded God? How *could* he do so? Man can only degrade God in his conceptions of Him. He may think meanly and poorly of God, instead of investing Him in his ideas with every perfection. And this is just what really took place. Man might have learned from Nature (for Nature is a revelation of God to a rational creature) the lesson of God's eternal power and Godhead, had he been so minded; His magnificence, His wisdom, His benevolence, are written in no obscure characters on the whole frame of the universe: "For the invisible things of Him from the creation of the world are clearly seen, being understood by the things that are made." But man could not, or rather he would not, rise to those lofty conceptions of God's character which Nature, studied with a simple and docile heart, furnishes. It is clear to common-sense that the watchmaker must be a far more wonderful being than the watch; yet man *would* not think of God as a Being infinitely raised above even the noblest works of His hands; he confounded Him with the creatures that were derived from Him, and allowed the religious instinct—the instinct of worship—to fasten upon them instead of the Creator. In a word, Idolatry (or the surrounding the creature with the attributes of the Creator) is the original, fundamental sin of man—the point of departure from which man started on his downward course until he reached the lowest depths of wickedness. And pray observe how, in the verses before us, the rapid deterioration of Idolatry (clearly showing the radical viciousness of its principle) is indicated "They changed the glory of the uncorruptible God into an image made like to corruptible man"—well, man is at all events the image and glory of God; and some forms of human character have been so lofty, so commanding, so generous, so attractive, that if *any* of the creatures might excusably be made a representative of the Most High in our minds, man might. But what shall we say of clothing with the attributes of God things lower than man in the scale of Creation? What shall we say of attributing some magical virtue, some mystical control over human affairs, to the ox, the hawk, the beetle? Yet to this point of utter debasement did Idolatry proceed: "They changed the glory of the incorruptible God into an image made like to . . . . birds, and four-footed beasts, and creeping things." And mark the awful result,—in which the Apostle recognizes, not the mere operation of a natural law, but a righteous retribution inflicted by a personal God: "Wherefore God gave them up to uncleanness." "For this cause God gave them up unto vile affections." Man had debased God in his conceptions of Him. And God, as the meet recompense of such dishonor done Him, really and actually debased man by abandoning him to the dominion of vices, the very mention of which freezes the blood of an upright man, and makes his hair stand on end.

And now to turn to account, for the purpose of our argument, this grand piece of Christian Philosophy. Man's point of departure for vice and a *downward* moral course is an unworthy and degrading conception of God. What is his point of departure for an *upward* moral course? What is the salient point, the spring, of all virtue? The Holy Scriptures make answer in no equivocal terms, "Faith,"—Faith in Christ, since it has pleased God to *reveal* His Son to us, but Faith ultimately in God, as the basis upon which every subsequent development of faith must be built. "Ye believe in God," said Our Lord to His disciples, ye have the foundation of true faith; now then go on to rear the superstructure: "Believe also in Me."

What then is faith in God? Let us seek to analyze it, and to see what processes of mind it involves. When directed toward God or Christ, faith takes the form of trust. (Luther said, somewhat too boldly and without qualification, that *all* faith was trust.) But how can we trust a person without a high conception of his character? The child trusts implicitly in its father—why? Because it thinks of its father as of a friend who loves it, who is able to help, and wise to counsel it. Specially, perhaps, because it thinks its father able to help. There is nothing which young children more readily give their parents credit for than power. The parent, however limited his resources may really be, is able, in their view of him, to extend protection to them under all circumstances, to extricate them from every difficulty, to make any arrangements for their comfort. Similarly, in all trust in God, there must be the inward apprehension that God is the Father of our spirits, that He cares for us tenderly, consults for us wisely, is able to help to the uttermost in every difficulty which can entangle us,—nay, has a reach of love, and wisdom, and power, to which it is impossible to set bounds. Once upon a time there was a poor heathen woman who remarkably exemplified this trust in God, and into the workings of whose mind, in the exercise of trust, a glimpse is given us. She had looked abroad upon Nature with a thoughtful eye. She had marked there that the wants of the meanest creatures are provided for; that He who rolls the planet on its course of fire, and streaks the western sky with glorious sunsets, stoops to paint the harebell that trembles on the heath, to feed the young raven, to cater even for the dogs. A Personage, of Whom she probably knew no more than that He claimed to be in immediate communication with God, and that He wrought every sort of cure in attestation of His claims, came into her neighborhood at a time when she was in great trouble from the seizure of her daughter by an evil spirit, who harassed his victim with fits and frenzies, very sad for any one to see, but most of all a mother. She came to this Personage, and implored Him to heal her daughter. But He was a great Jewish Prophet, and she a poor benighted heathen; and it pleased Him to intimate as much, first by turning a deaf ear to her, and then, when her clamor extorted from Him some words, by the repelling answer that God's mercies were for His chosen people, for the children of His household, not for heathen dogs. But from the study of His works she had learned God too well to be discouraged by this chilling response. "Dogs"—be it so; but did not the great Father of all make provision even for dogs? was not even good food, the remnants of the children's bread, often thrown to the dogs in the households of the rich? a proof this that God could never spurn from Him even the lowest creatures of His hand. Her faith, as well it might, received a solemn commendation and recompense from the Saviour of the world. But what *was* her faith? It was simply a high idea of God's tender care for all His creatures, drawn from a devout observation of His ways in Nature and Providence, and engendering a deep trust in His goodness, a trust which was proof against all discouragement—which held its ground in her heart, when very severely tried. Admirable woman! she cherished those great notions of our Heavenly Father, and that unswerving trust in Him, which is the point of departure for all virtue, just as a lack of these great notions, and of the trust which they engender, is the point of departure for all vice.

The Lesson which we have thus arrived at is taught us very emphatically by the Lord's Prayer. I assume that one grand object of that Prayer is to form the character of the petitioner to that Holiness, without which no man shall see the Lord. Now what is the first petition? It is a prayer that God's character and attributes may be by us worthily conceived of; that His Name (by which is meant His character and attributes) may be hallowed, regarded with profoundest reverence, thought of as most excellent in power, wisdom, and love. The man who is bent upon the pursuit of righteousness will pray for this before other things, because this worthy conception of God must be the source of faith, and the foundation of all virtue and goodness, in the heart of a rational creature.

Seek, then, my reader—this is the great lesson of the present chapter—seek to feed and nourish in your mind great conceptions of Him, with Whom you have to do. Expand and exalt your notions of Him by every means in your power.

"What are these means?" you will naturally ask. And for an answer I refer you to those passages of Scripture, which have just been passed under review. The Apostle says that the invisible things of God, even His eternal power and Godhead, "are clearly seen from the creation of the world" (i. e., God's creation of the world is the source from which true information respecting His lofty attributes may be gained), "so that they" (the Gentiles) "are without excuse," because the lessons which they might have learned of God from Nature are quite sufficient to have condemned their idolatries. And the Psalmist only throws the same truth into another form, when he says, "The heavens declare the glory of God, and the firmament showeth His handiwork." And to the same effect are many of the addresses of the Almighty to Job, who was certainly not one of the chosen people, and who is reasoned with therefore from God's mighty works in Nature, not from the Old Testament Revelation. And as an *example* of a Gentile's actually learning precious truth respecting God's character and attributes from His dealings in Providence, if not in Nature, we have the Syrophœnician in the Gospel. Jews and Christians too often seem to think that they put honor upon the particular revelations which God has made to them, by disparaging and neglecting the revelation which He has made to the Gentiles in common with them. But why, because superior edification and clearer light are to be had from our own Bible, are we to look down upon the edification and light which are to be derived from the Bible of the Gentiles? Might we not on the same principle neglect the Old Testament, because the New is of superior importance? But what is the case as regards the Old and New Testament—the Bible of the Jews, as it might be called, and the Bible of the Christians? I appeal to any devout and well-read student of Holy Scripture—is not the Old Testament, when read in the light of the New, full of interest and edification, so that Leah is hardly surpassed by Rachel—the elder sister is nearly as lovely and as attractive as the younger? Nay, is it not the *Old* Testament, of which the Apostle says that it is able to make us wise unto salvation through faith that is in Christ Jesus? Now why may not the same reasoning be applied to the Gentiles' Bible—the Revelation of God which existed long before the Law and the Prophets? Why may we not, under the combined light of the Old and New Testaments, learn grand and glorious lessons, lessons soul-elevating and soul-edifying, from the Book of Nature and the Book of Providence? What are our Blessed Lord's Parables (the highest form, I suppose, of all religious teaching), but sermons preached, not from texts of the Old Testament, but from texts in Nature and Providence? Christ's texts do not run in this style, "In the fifteenth chapter of the Book of Deuteronomy, and the third verse;" but in this, "A sower went out to sow his seed;" "A certain man had two sons;" "Consider the lilies of the field, how they grow;" "Behold the fowls of the air . . . your Heavenly Father feedeth them" (it really seems as if the poor Syrophœnician woman had heard that sermon upon the fowls of the air—at all events she laid to heart its teaching). And remember how much more largely Nature has been expounded, how much better she is understood now, than in the days when that poor heathen woman drew such precious lessons from her. Then I say, if you would nourish in your heart high notions of God, consider the lilies of the field, which His hand paints with such beautiful colors that Solomon's robe of state is a coarse garment in comparison of them. Consider the fowls of the air, for whose wants this Almighty Householder makes provision, and whose death-warrant He must sign before one of them can fall to the ground. Consider the trees, and their marvellous resuscitation in the spring from the bleakness and deadness of winter, a spectacle of which it is on record that the very thought of such a process going on all over the world was made the instrument[1] of converting a soul. Consider the stars, with which the vast reaches of the midnight sky are everywhere spangled—many of them, it is supposed, the suns of other systems, ministering to those sys-

[1] See "The Conversations and Letters of Brother Lawrence." [Masters.] "He told me . . . . that in the winter, seeing a tree stripped of its leaves, and considering that within a little time the leaves would be renewed, and after that the flowers and fruit appear, he received a high view of the Providence and power of God, which has never since been effaced from his soul. That this had perfectly set him loose from the world, and kindled in him such a love for God, that he could not tell whether it had increased in above forty years that he had lived since."

tems light and warmth, as our sun does to our system. Consider the wonderful architecture of the universe, and the admirable skill with which the Creator has furnished and decorated His great mansion. Occupy your thoughts with the wonderful instances of wise and beneficent design which have been so admirably pointed out by Paley[1] and others, and to which the modern advancement of science is continually contributing fresh stores. And then consider, the work being so skilful, so magnificent, and adjusted to so many beneficent purposes, how infinitely more wise and grand and beneficent the Maker of it must be.—Perhaps you say disdainfully, "This is a mere truth of Natural Religion." So it is; but it is a truth by which, if they would make more use of it, and lay it more to heart, the disciples of Revealed Religion might be wonderfully edified. *For what they most need, what lies at the very foundation of their faith, is an exalted conception of God.* And whence shall they draw this conception in all its purity and strength but from the book in which God is not described only, but visibly illustrated to the observing eye, and the understanding heart—the book of Nature? Only, when you walk abroad along the hedgerows, or by the side of the stream, or over the heath-clad moor,

[1] For I cannot at all sympathize with that depreciation of Paley's line of argument, which is so much in vogue nowadays, and to which I regret to see that that most brilliant and profound of orators, the Bishop of Peterborough, has condescended (*Sermon before the British Association in Norwich Cathedral*, 1868). Because we have (or think we have) found out "a more excellent way" of defending Revealed Religion, this is no reason why we should abolish the lines of defence reared by our ancestors.

do so in a devout spirit, a spirit turned toward God for the purpose of communion with Him, and your mind shall expand as you contemplate His wonders; as a poet of our own hath said, you shall

> "Find tongues in trees, books in the running brooks,
> Sermons in stones, and good in every thing."

CHAPTER V.

THE EXPERIMENTAL KNOWLEDGE OF GOD THE END OF ALL CHRISTIAN ENDEAVOR.

"*Increasing in the knowledge of God.*"—Col. i. 10.

IN the last chapter we considered what is the point of departure in the attainment of Holiness, the direction in which our faces should be set, if we would reach that goal. The next point with which we shall deal is the end which is to be kept in view in all Christian endeavor. It is for want of keeping this end steadily before them that many well-meaning persons waste so much time and energy, and make so little progress. The fact is, their efforts are misdirected. They are strongly impressed with the necessity of religion, and with the desire of being religious, without perceiving clearly in what religion consists. They confound the means of being religious, or the effects of true religion, with its life and soul, and rest satisfied if their conduct exhibits these means and some of these effects. Much the same confusion of thought as if in agriculture a man should take digging, manuring, and pruning, or blossoming and fruit-bearing, to be the life of a tree, whereas the one are means to keep the tree alive, and the other evidences of its being alive. What, then, is the life and soul of true religion? What the one point, at which all religious efforts are to be directed? When once we perceive this distinctly, all the circumstantials of the spiritual life, the means of cultivating it, the fruits to be looked for from it, will fall into their right place in our minds. This and the following chapter will be devoted to giving an answer to this question.

The life of true Religion, then, is an experimental knowledge (I do not like hard words, still less the technical language of theological parties, let us say rather, a heart-knowledge) of God—such a thorough appreciation of the excellence and beauty of His character as really contents and satisfies the soul, even when earthly sources of happiness fail. I say, which *satisfies* the soul; understand that well; for this satisfaction is the test of the knowledge being of the right sort. St. Philip on a certain occasion said (not knowing what he said, probably as ignorant of the depth and reach of his words as was Caiaphas in his unconscious prophecy), "Lord, show us the Father, and it sufficeth us." No earthly source of happiness *does* suffice. The objects of human desire and ambition are very fair, and at a distance promise very well to him who can come up with them. But the pursuit of them (and the whole natural life of man is one long pursuit) is like the countryman's chase after the rainbow. He thought that one limb of the bright arch rested in the field close to him, but when he had cleared the hedge, and come up to the spot on which it seemed to rest, the rainbow had adjourned into another field. Even so these various earthly objects of desire or ambition, one after another, disappoint those who attain them; their prismatic colors all vanish when we come up close to them, they are found to have their anxieties and their troubles (not the least of which is the precarious tenure of them), and some new rainbow is seen ahead, two or three fields off, to lure us into a pursuit which turns out to be as fruitless as the former. Must it ever be so? Is there no really satisfactory object in which the soul of man may find a full and perfect contentment? Assuredly there is. Our Creator does not mock and baffle us by implanting strong instincts in our Nature, and great yearnings after happiness, which have nothing corresponding to them. In the knowledge of God, in the appreciation of God, in the enjoyment of God, in communion with God, but in nothing short of this, man can find rest. All ordinances, even the Holy Eucharist, which is the highest of all, are only means to this Communion. And all good works, in any high sense of the word, are only the fruits of this Communion.

Observe now that this knowledge of God is, indeed, the end of ends, to which every other part of the religious system, even those which in themselves are most essential, is subordinated. It is the end of the atoning and interceding work of our dear Lord and Master, the aim of His whole priestly function. For what did Christ die, but to reconcile sinners unto God? For what does He intercede, but to introduce sinners to God, to bring them into living communion with His Father? The precious Death and the glorious Intercession were only the removal of barriers, which, had they been allowed to remain in the way, must have precluded communion with God forever. Our Blessed Lord's Death and His Intercession are both parts of His Mediation. And what is meant by His Mediation? Is it not this, that, in our present state, the sin that is in us prevents our coming to God, and enjoying communion with Him, except through our great Representative, Who endured for us all the curse, and fulfilled for us all the righteousness, of the Law? Any true knowledge of God, independently of Christ, must frighten us from Him, instead of drawing us toward Him. For God is infinitely holy, and in His holiness is a consuming fire to sinners approaching Him otherwise than through a Mediator. But all this implies that the Mediation of Christ is itself, as, indeed, the word denotes, a means to an end, which end is communion with God, such a knowledge of Him as involves love of Him and delight in Him.

It may be asked, indeed, by a thoughtful listener, whether Our Lord, in indicating the great commandment of the Law, and whether the structure of the Decalogue, on which He founds what He says, does not give us *two* ends of religious endeavor rather than one, the love of our neighbor as well as the love of God, "Thou shalt love thy neighbor as thyself." But the answer to this is very obvious. Man is so slow at perceiving what is wrapped up in the principles he admits, so backward in carrying those principles into effect, that the practices which flow from the principles need pressing no less than the principles themselves. Thus faith, if genuine, will as certainly produce good works, as a tree, if alive, will certainly produce fruit. And hence it might be thought that, as faith will carry with it good works, it is sufficient to press faith, and leave the works to follow in natural course. But the Scriptures everywhere show us (if, indeed, our own knowledge of the human heart does not show us sufficiently without the Scriptures) that this omission cannot safely be made. Duty must be pressed distinctly and explicitly, not left to be implied in the motives from which it is to proceed. And so in the case before us. Our Lord, when asked about the relative importance of the Commandments, could not safely make answer without some explicit reference to the Second Table of the Law. Yet He does not hereby deny that the love of God, if genuine, includes and embraces that of our neighbor. In fact, though each needs to be explicitly mentioned, they are not two independent commandments. We are to love our neighbor for God and in God, because God has created and redeemed him (no less than ourselves); we are to see in him God's handiwork, and a soul redeemed by God, and to love him *as such.* And this only, and no lower regard, constitutes Christian Love.

Now, if we are bent upon becoming holy, it is of the greatest moment to us to perceive that the life of true Religion consists in the experimental knowledge and love of God. Unity of aim is a great point in the Christian Life. We make no advance, we can make none, while we are occupied in a variety of endeavors which have no common principle or end; while we are busied about many things, doing here a little and there a little in the way of Religion, without seeking, in all that we do, "the one thing" supremely needful. Moreover, the keeping before us steadily of the true end will show us what religious exercises are most worth cultivating, and upon what our time and labor will be always well bestowed.

These will be the exercises which go most directly, and with least circuitousness, to the great end.

As thus—

(1) The knowledge of God is gained, as the knowledge of man is gained, by living much with Him. If we only come across a man occasionally, and in public, and see nothing of him in his private and domestic life, we cannot be said to know him. All the knowledge of God which many professing Christians have is derived from a formal salute which they make to Him in their prayers, when they rise up in the morning and lie down at night. While this state of things lasts, no great progress in the Christian Life can possibly be made. No progress *would* be made, even if they were to offer stated prayer seven times a day, instead of twice. But try to draw down God into your daily work; consult Him about it; offer it to Him as a contribution to His Service; ask Him to help you in it; ask Him to bless it; do it as to the Lord and not unto men; refer to Him in your temptations; seek a refuge under the shadow of His wings until the tyranny of temptation be overpast; go back *at once* to His bosom, when you are conscious of a departure from Him, not waiting till night to confess it, lest meanwhile the night of death should overtake you, or at best you should lose time in your spiritual course; in short, walk hand in hand with God through life (as a little child walks hand in hand with its father over some dangerous and thorny road), dreading above all things to quit His side, and assured that, as soon as you do so, you will fall into mischief and trouble; seek not so much to pray as to live in an *atmosphere* of prayer, lifting up your heart momentarily to Him

in varied expressions of devotion as the various occasions of life may prompt, adoring Him, thanking Him, resigning your will to Him many times a day, and more or less all day; and you shall thus, as you advance in this practice, as it becomes more and more habitual to you, increase in that knowledge of God which fully contents and satisfies the soul.

(2) Again; it is obvious that the knowledge of God of which we speak may be obtained from studying His mind as it is given us in the Holy Scriptures. We may be said to know an author, when we have so carefully and constantly read his works as to imbibe his spirit. A direct step, therefore, to the knowledge we are in search of, may be made by what our Ordinal calls "daily reading and weighing of the Scriptures"—not "reading" merely, but "weighing," thinking over them, applying them to our own case, judging ourselves by the standard they set up, seeking to hear God's voice in them, treasuring them up in our hearts against the hour of need as infallible oracles. It is through His Word that God speaks to us, as it is through Prayer that we speak to God; for which reason he who would cultivate acquaintance with God must cultivate a taste for the Holy Scriptures—I do not mean, of course, a literary or antiquarian taste (though as a mere piece of ancient literature the Bible is the most wonderful book in the world), but a devotional taste; he must aim at being able to say with the Psalmist, "Oh, how sweet are Thy words unto my taste! yea, sweeter than honey to my mouth! Oh, how I love Thy law! all the day long is my study in it." Observe, "all the day long." My mind, in which it is stored up, is always recurring to it in the

intervals of business, turning it over with fresh inquiry into its significance, finding new illustrations of its truth in Nature, in human life, in my own experience. There is a study of Scripture which is analogous to ejaculatory prayer—not a stated study (though of course the stated study of it may not be neglected), but a study which inweaves the Word into the daily life of the Christian, a rumination which can be carried on without book, and which is more or less continual.

(3) Again; if sanctity stands in the knowledge of God, surely the discipline of life will very much contribute, under God's blessing, toward sanctity. If a man has had no dealings with us personally, though we may have heard of him, and he may be no stranger to us by reputation, we cannot be said to *know* him. But if transactions of many different sorts pass between us, his character then transpires, and his ways reveal themselves to us. Now our Heavenly Father comes up close to us, if He sees that we are resolutely bent on giving our hearts to Him, and deals with us, "in all the changing scenes of life, in trouble and in joy." So long as people desire to hold Him at arm's length, He only sweeps round the circumference of their existence; but when they desire to have Him in their hearts, He advances into the centre of their life. He trains them for glory by what is called their fortunes, by reverses, by tears, by trials, by manifold temptations, by touching them in their sensitive part, sometimes by a sunshine of prosperity, which makes their heart expand in gratitude to Him. Those, then, who desire to have a practical and experimental, as distinct from a speculative knowledge of Him, will

study Him in these His dealings; they will try to discern the lesson of every part of their own experience, if haply it may teach them something of Him with Whom they have to do, and will thus have His wisdom, power, and love, impressed upon them in a way, in which nothing short of experience can impress.

We will conclude this chapter by observing that increase in the knowledge of God, as it characterizes the true Christian's present course, so will it be his business throughout eternity. For we are not to conceive of a glorified saint as if he were stereotyped in a certain measure of Light and Love, and could advance no farther than to a certain point in the knowledge of God. Our nature seems to be so constituted as not to acquiesce in a particular measure of knowledge on any subject; we are not made to be stationary; progress toward a goal, which yet we never can reach, seems to be one essential condition of our happiness. And why, as God is infinite, and His resources of wisdom, power, and love, are inexhaustible, may not a blessed eternity be spent in fresh discoveries of His glory, each of which will throw preceding discoveries into the shade, and serve as a new theme of adoration and praise? O great soul of man, made for the Infinite, made for the apprehension of the Heavenly Father in all the beauty of His holiness and in all the sweetness of His love, what a wrong doest thou to thyself and to thine own capacities, by grovelling among low and unclean desires, as among the swine, and feeding upon the husks of mere momentary enjoyments! Reader, thou hast one of these treasures, an immortal spirit, intrusted to thy charge. The

Eternal Son of God prized it so highly that He stooped to earth to gather it up, shed His Blood to ransom it, offers His Spirit to sanctify it, designs to place it as a jewel in His Redemption Crown. Will you, through love of sin, or mere carelessness and frivolity, forfeit it again? Will you unfold its great capacities under the guidance of His Spirit; or will you allow it to run to waste, like those many seeds in Nature, which are never quickened into life? And what is to repay thee for the loss of it? Hear and weigh the solemn words, "What shall it profit a man, if he shall gain the whole world, and lose his own soul?"

CHAPTER VI.

THE END OF THE COMMANDMENT, AND THE IMPORTANCE OF KEEPING IT IN VIEW.

"*Now the end of the commandment is charity out of a pure heart, and of a good conscience, and of faith unfeigned: from which some having swerved, have turned aside unto vain jangling.*"—1 TIM. i. 5, 6.

THERE is a metaphor in these words (more apparent in the original than in the translation), drawn from the subject of archery. The word rendered "swerving" denotes the missing or going wide of the point at which an arrow is aimed. By "the commandment" is probably meant the whole code of God's Precepts, whether under the Law or the Gospel. These precepts are very numerous; but many as they are, they may all be reduced under two great heads—nay, they may all be summarized under *one* head, Charity or Love. The aim of every commandment, of the whole code of Precepts, is love to God and man, love flowing out of a heart purified by faith in Christ's Blood, and sanctified by Christ's Spirit, and out of a conscience which makes echo that the heart is indeed thus purified and sanctified. Those religious teachers who do not place this before them as the aim of all Divine Precept, are apt to go very wide of the mark, and to engage their listeners with unprofitable controversial questions. The same idea as to the main bearing of Divine Precept is given us by Our Lord in His answer to the lawyer's question, "Master, which is the great commandment in the law? Jesus said unto him, Thou shalt love the Lord thy God with all thy heart, and with all thy soul, and with all thy mind. This is the first and great commandment. And the second is like unto it, Thou shalt love thy neighbor as thyself. On these two commandments hang all the Law and the Prophets." (The imagery here is taken from the custom of fixing in the brickwork of Oriental houses large nails, upon which to suspend various domestic utensils.) And St. Paul in his Epistle to the Romans has the same idea in yet another form: "Owe no man any thing, but to love one another: for he that loveth another hath fulfilled the Law. . . . Love worketh no ill to his neighbor; therefore Love is the fulfilling of the Law." Thus Love is represented in Holy Scripture, sometimes as the contents or filling up of God's precepts, sometimes as the mark or butt to which every precept is directed, sometimes again, as the stay and support upon which every precept is suspended. It is a great testimony to the importance of the doctrine thus announced, that it is thrice solemnly reiterated in different parts of Holy Scripture, and under different forms of expression.

It is obvious that, in order to solid proficiency in any kind of art, the student must first be furnished with a clear answer to the question, What is the object—the end to be reached? Take the art of oratory, for instance. What (in brief) is the thing to be done by the orator, the end at which he must aim? Let us say that it is to persuade the audience to adopt or refrain from a certain course of action. If he can persuade them to do what he advises, he hits the mark, he reaches the end of the art—in a word, he succeeds. But if, after having heard him, they act in a way opposite to that which he recommends, he goes wide of the mark—his speech is a failure. And this is a good subject to draw the instance from, because as a fact both speakers and hearers often do make much the same mistake as to oratory, which, as I shall presently show, is universally made as to Religion. Too often, for example, is a fine sermon thought to be, not that which gives a spur to the wills of the hearers, not that which induces them to set about reforming their lives, and becoming good people, but that which merely explains a difficult text of the Bible, or which goes toward settling a controversial question, or which, not even possessing merits as high as these, has merely fine language and flowers of rhetoric to recommend it. Now it is clear that the perception of the true end is the first step toward setting the practice right. I have done something toward rectifying my preaching, if I have settled it in my own mind that, on the one hand, I shall fail utterly, unless I send the audience away with a desire for, and an impulse toward, spiritual improvement, and that, on the other, I shall succeed perfectly, if I do send them away with such a desire and impulse, even if my sermon should settle no controversy, should explain no merely speculative difficulty, and should be absolutely wanting in fine words and in all the graces of style. St. John was a true orator in his old age, when from his infirmities he was unable to say no more than this, "Little children, love one another," because the antecedents of that holy and venerable Bishop, and the deep and living sympathy with which he uttered the words, really moved the hearers to comply with the precept, and their feuds sank to rest at the sound of his voice.

Let us take an instance from another art, where there may perhaps be some *doubt* as to what should be the artist's object. What is the end of painting, the aim which the painter must set before him? Is it to deceive the spectator, to give him a false impression, to make him imagine that the painted object is a real one? It would seem that the ancients thought so from the story current among them of the trial of skill between Zeuxis and Parrhasius, in which one of them painted a bunch of grapes so like nature, that the birds came and pecked at them, and the other a curtain so like real drapery, that his brother artist called on him to draw the curtain and exhibit his picture. Or is the end of painting not to deceive, but to please the spectator by a faithful imitation of Nature—an end which is incompatible with deception; for if the spectator is to be affected with pleasure by the fidelity of an imitation, he must, of course, be aware that it *is* an imitation, and not the reality? And, again, *how* is Nature to be imitated by the painter? Servilely, and in a matter-of-fact way, line upon line, feature by feature? Or shall we say rather that there is a soul in Nature, a soul in every countenance, ay, and a soul in every landscape, which struggles for a fuller development, and to which it is the painter's business to give expression? In other words, is a photograph the very highest style of imitative art, because it is true in the letter? or is a portrait of Raffaelle's or Murillo's infinitely higher than any photograph can be, because it is true not so much in the letter as in the spirit? It is not to my point to answer these questions, but only to call attention to the fact that they may be asked, and answered differently. And an artist who intends to paint successfully must have a clear answer to them in his mind before he begins. He must resolve himself on the question, "What is the true object of my art? Is it to produce deception? Is it to please persons by a faithful imitation of Nature? And if so, what *is* a faithful imitation? Is it a servile copy, like the Chinese imitation of pottery, which reproduces the flaws and the cracks; or is it the development of a feature which in the original seems to yearn for expression?" If this point be not settled at the beginning, he is certain to go astray in the execution.

The above illustrations will not be thrown away, if they tend in any mind to clear up the position which we are endeavoring to establish. As in the arts, so also in the pursuit of Holiness, or in other words, in the spiritual life, *there is an end;* and it is all-important that they who would be proficients in the spiritual life should discern clearly what this end is, and hold it steadily before them in their every endeavor. The end is love—supreme love, with all the powers of the soul, to God—and such love to our brethren as we bear to ourselves—this love to be engendered by a living faith in what God has done for us, a faith which sets free the heart both from a sense of guilt and from a love of sin, and which thus sets the conscience at ease. If this love is in some measure yielded both to God and man, the object of true religion is attained. If this love is *not* produced and maintained in the soul, we fail altogether in true Religion, and that, though we may have been very busy *about* Religion, may have put up many prayers, heard many sermons, attended many sacraments, assisted in many philanthropic enterprises.

Some, perhaps, will ask, and not without surprise, "Are not Prayers, and Scripture Readings, and Sermons, are not even Sacraments and good works, true Religion?" No; not if you will think accurately on the subject, without confusing the relations of the various parts of the Religious system. Prayer and Scripture Reading, and Sermons, and Sacraments, are means to true Religion; and as they are means of Divine appointment, they are sure, if faithfully and devoutly used, to conduce to the end. But for all that, they are *not* the end; and to regard them as such is a mischievous confusion of thought, which may very possibly disturb our spiritual aim, and make us shoot very wide of the mark. It is true, no doubt, that the religious exercises we have specified are absolutely essential (in all cases where they may be had) to the spiritual life. But even this fact does not take them out of the category of means, and make them ends. A scaffolding is the means of building a house; nay, more, it is an essential means; for how could the upper stories ever be raised without a scaffolding? But in material things of this kind, no one ever mistakes the means for the end. No one ever confounds the house with the scaffolding, or imagines that the object of a builder is achieved, if nothing should ever be exhibited to the eye *but* scaffolding, if there be no foundation dug, and no layers of bricks begin to rise above the earth. But in matters spiritual there are hundreds who are satisfied with themselves, if they exhibit day by day nothing but a religious apparatus, if they have literally nothing to show but prayers duly and attentively said, Church duly attended, Sacraments periodically and solemnly received. And others there are, who confound the *fruits* of Religion with Religion itself—who, because they bear a part in good works, help good objects, devote some time and money to the relief of the poor, are perfectly satisfied with these external symptoms of spirituality, and never stop to inquire whether they are in deed and in truth spiritual. But alas! it is too possible to be useful in many ways, without being actuated in what we do by love to God or love to man, without a sincere desire to please and glorify our Creator, or to serve and benefit those who were made in His image, and redeemed by His Son's Blood.

See now how the keeping the end of the religious life steadily before us gives a right direction to effort, and simplifies our work.

1. And, first, how it gives a right direction to effort. Energy is so valuable a thing that it is melancholy to think of any of it being thrown away, and running to waste. In religious and moral life, more especially, we all manifest so little energy, that it is necessary to make every effort as telling as possible, so as to husband what energy we have. And no effort can be telling, unless it be bestowed in the right quarter. Now, if the great end of all Religion be the love of God, and of man for God's sake, this shows in what quarter our efforts should be directed.

It is not so much the thing done, as the spirit in which it is done, which is of such great moment. For love is an affection of the heart and will, and we know that very small tokens, the merest trifles, will evince it; and that, when it is evinced, it has a peculiar power of winning its way both with God and man. Suppose a great fortune laid out in building churches, or relieving the poor, under the pressure of servile fear, and with the design of expiating sin, or a great philanthropic enterprise inaugurated and maintained from ambitious motives; can it be supposed that such acts, however it may please Him to bless the effects of them, go for any thing with God as regards the doer of them? And, on the other hand, suppose some very simple, commonplace action, something not going at all beyond the circle of routine and daily duty, done with a grateful, affectionate feeling toward God, and from a simple desire to please Him, and to win His approval—can it be supposed that such an action, however trifling in itself, does *not* go for something, nay, for much, with God? The love of Him with all the heart, and mind, and soul, and strength, is "the first and great commandment." One movement of that love gives to the commonest action the fragrance of a sacrifice; while, without one movement of it, the costliest offering must of necessity be rejected. "If a man should give all the substance of his house for love, it would utterly be contemned."

And does not love win its way also with man, who is made in the Image of God? A wealthy person, who only condescends to relieve the poor out of his abundance, without feeling or expressing sympathy with them, finds thereby no door of access to their hearts, though they may be glad enough to avail themselves of his munificence. While, on the other hand, one who has little or nothing to *give* the poor, but visits them with evident interest in their condition, and words and looks expressive of that interest, is sure to insinuate himself into their confidence and affection. The moral of all which is, that if we would bestow our efforts in the spiritual life well and wisely, we need not so much seek to do something religious, as *to do ordinary things in a religious manner*, cultivating high and loving thoughts of God while we do our work, and seeking to do it well, where no eyes are upon us, from the view of pleasing Him; and in all services to our fellow-men thinking of the Image of God, which lies hidden and overlaid with rubbish in their souls, as in ours, and of the enormous price of Christ's Blood, which was paid down for all, showing how high must have been God's estimation of each of them. I believe we shall never regret any amount of pains taken in doing common things as unto the Lord, and in striving to evince love to Him by means of them.

2. Finally; the keeping before us steadily the love of God and man as our great end wonderfully *simplifies* our work; abbreviates it, if I may so express myself, and saves us the toil of many a circuitous route. Say that I have sinned to-day, come miserably short of my good resolutions, gone back from grace. What is to be done now? Nature prompts me to delay my return to my Heavenly Father, under the plea that it is a very arduous and elaborate business, which cannot be achieved in a short time. Nature says that ap-

proaches must be thrown up by prayers, and fastings, and ordinances, before we can come at the footstool of an offended God; that, moreover, we must draw near to Him after the established and methodized system, humbling ourselves first, and dreading His vengeance, then lifting up our heads in hope, and finally, after such due preparation, offering our prayer for mercy. Now is not all this going round, when we might go direct to the point at once? And if this policy is made a plea for delay in returning, is it not most hazardous, inasmuch as only the present moment of life is ours for certain? What saith the Scripture? "Her sins, which are many, are forgiven; *for she loved much.*" A loving confidence in the God we have offended, though not of course in any shape meritorious, is the key to his heart, the key which unlocks the treasury of His grace. What is the *object* in all religion? What is the thing to be done, the end to be arrived at? "Love out of a pure heart, and of a good conscience, and of faith unfeigned." Then would it not be wiser, shorter, better, to make straight for this end at once? Nature whispers that, having been unfaithful to Him, I ought to go to God in tears. So I ought; but if the tears were not shed by love, they would not be acceptable. Then, with a perfect confidence in the power of the Blood of Christ to wash away this (as every other) stain from the conscience, let me walk straight up to my Heavenly Father with the utmost amount of filial affection, filial confidence, filial yearning, which I can muster. My filial relationship to Him cannot be ruptured by my sin. And God's fatherly compassion, founded upon that relationship, cannot be expunged from His heart, even should His holiness and justice oblige Him to banish me. Then let me take my stand upon that compassion which prompted the gift of Christ for me, and plead it with Him, and tell Him that I want a free forgiveness, in order that I may return again to His guidance with as little delay as may be. Tears will be in the way to flow when I think upon His much-abused love, and try my best to return it. For great are His gifts to the slightest exercise of confidence on the part of His children. Rich is His answer to the prayer, in which He hears even a single note of filial sentiment. When the prodigal is yet a great way off, the father sees him, and runs, and falls on his neck and kisses him. Verily we do Him wrong to think that He, Who hath given up His Son for us all, requires laborious preparations before we can approach Him, or can be pleased with any thing short of love. Balak's three times seven altars and seven rams were quite beside the mark, as a means of winning the Divine acceptance. He asked[1] (and it is the question which Nature always asks), "Wherewith shall I come before the Lord, and bow myself before the high God? Shall I come before Him with burnt-offerings, with calves of a year old? Will the Lord be pleased with thousands of rams, or with ten thousands

[1] I have taken Bishop Butler's view of the meaning of this passage in Micah (vi. 5, 6), without, however, being ignorant of what is to be said against it. According to this view, there is no break between *v.* 5 and 6; but *vv.* 6, 7 give Balak's "consultation," and *v.* 8, "what Balaam, the son of Beor, answered him." It makes no difference to my argument, whether this, or the contrary view, be adopted. Either way, the lesson of *vv.* 6, 7, 8, is just the same.

of rivers of oil?" And how was he answered by the Prophet?—that love to man, and an humble affectionate trust in God, is the only available sacrifice. "He hath showed thee, O man, what is good; and what doth the Lord require of thee, but to do justly, and to love mercy, and to walk humbly with thy God?"

CHAPTER VII.

OF THE VARIOUS SENTIMENTS EMBRACED IN THE LOVE OF GOD.

"*Thou shalt love the Lord thy God with all thy heart, and with all thy soul, and with all thy strength, and with all thy mind.*"—LUKE x. 27.

AN over-subtle scrutiny of the words of a sentence sometimes impairs our perception of its force. Nor are the inspired sentences of Holy Scripture exceptions to this rule. As by dissecting a dead body in an anatomy-school you could gain no notion of the contour, general bearing, and power of the living body; as by bringing a microscope to bear upon the vein of an insect's wing you could form no just conception of that insect, as it disports itself in the summer sun; so by entering with too great minuteness into the language of Holy Scripture, it is possible to miss (or at least to apprehend but feebly) its great purport. Accordingly, I do not propose to draw any fanciful distinctions between the several faculties here specified as "the heart," "the soul," "the strength," and "the mind." The great scope of the precept obviously is that we should love God with all our powers. Whatever fibres there are in our nature, by which we cling and cleave to those around us, these fibres must all throw themselves out toward Him, and embrace Him as their first object.

Yet without appropriating any distinct force to each of the words of which our text is made up, we may remark generally in illustration of it that there are several senses in which the word "love" is used, or rather several kinds of love, between which we need not hesitate to draw a distinction, because such a distinction rests upon a real and palpable difference.

We saw in our last Chapter that the love of God is the sum and substance of all true Religion, and that in the pursuit of Holiness this love and the exercise of it must be kept steadily before us as our end. The love of God, then, in its different varieties, demands some amount of study from all who would follow after Holiness, and it will not be giving it too prominent a place in our argument if we devote to it several Chapters. In the present Chapter we will trace only the divisions of the subject, taking up afterward more fully any of those divisions which it seems most necessary to enlarge upon.

1. The first idea which starts into the mind at the mention of the word "love," the earliest form in which love presents itself to us, is that of natural affection. The little child loves its parents, clings to its mother, runs to welcome its father on his return home—this is with us all the earliest exercise of love. This exercise of love is without deliberation, without reason; it wells up spontaneously from the hidden depths of Nature. It has no moral esteem in it; it would be felt as much toward a bad parent as a good (supposing him, that is, not to be altogether bad *as* a parent,

which even the worst men seldom are). It has no gratitude in it; for it is experienced by children too young to appreciate the enormous debt which is due to a parent. And it has no benevolence in it; there is no desire in the child's mind of succoring the parents or rendering them assistance; nay, the idea that a parent can *need* any assistance is as far as possible from the minds of very young children, who usually conceive their parents to be omnipotent. In short, this love is an instinct, seated in Nature, and arising in some mysterious way (of which we can give no account) from the relationship between parent and child. The same instinct is found in an incipient and crude state among animals. In virtue of it the chickens seek the shelter and warmth of their mother's outspread wings. But in man this instinct, being kneaded up with the spirit or reason, becomes developed and spiritualized, and endures long after the age of childhood has passed away.

Now the question is, whether this love of natural affection is capable of being exercised toward Almighty God—is one of the forms in which we are exhorted to love Him? And the answer is, that it plainly is so. The Apostle to the Hebrews calls God "the Father of our spirits." And it was the peculiar mission of Our Blessed Lord to reveal and declare that most comfortable truth, the Paternity of God. Observe how the terms "your Father which is in heaven," "your Father," "thy Father which is in secret, which seeth in secret," "your heavenly Father," interpenetrate the Sermon on the Mount; how they are continually reappearing, as if they were the warp of the divine discourse.

Now this relationship to God is altogether peculiar to man, or at all events, if shared by him with other creatures, shared only with the Angels. The lower animals are God's *creatures*. And it cannot be denied that there is a tie of tenderness which, in virtue of this lower relationship, binds even them to their Creator, and gives them a place in His heart. Witness passages like these, which testify to such a tie:— "God remembered Noah and every living thing, and *all the cattle which was with him in the ark;*" "Should not I spare Nineveh, that great city wherein are more than sixscore thousand persons that cannot discern between their right hand and their left hand, and also *much cattle?*" "He giveth to the beast his fôod, and to the young ravens which cry;" "Are not five sparrows sold for two farthings? and *not one of them is forgotten before God.*" We find some echo of *this* sentiment of the Divine Mind in the tenderness of the artist or artisan to his own productions? Could a poet endure to burn the poem, or a sculptor to shiver the statue, or a mechanic to break the machinery, on which he had bestowed much skill, labor, and time? But the sentiment toward a production is of a lower grade and less tender than that toward offspring; and, "we," says St. Paul to the Athenians, quoting and adopting the words of a heathen poet, "*are His offspring.*" He is "the Father of our spirits;" the Father especially of that faculty in us which is capable of responding to His appeals and holding intercourse with Him—the reason or spirit. The power of moral choice, the conscience, the capacity of conversing with God in prayer, these are all scintillations from God's own uncreated essence.

Now the first love which God requires from us must flow from the recognition of this relationship between us and Himself, which, obscured as it had been by idolatry and the manifold corruptions of the human heart, it was one great object of the Gospel to bring to light and announce in the most explicit manner. Love indeed, the warmest love, is due to God from us on other grounds, on the ground of His mercy and loving-kindness, and on the ground of the intrinsic excellence and perfection of His character. But none of the more rational and deliberate exercises of affection can dispense us from the instinct which arises from the simple relationship subsisting between Him and us. What would be thought of a son, whose entire feeling to his father was expressed thus: "I love you because you have been so kind to me, and because you are so excellent a man." These are most rational grounds of love, but the parent would probably wish to hear alleged as well as these: "I love you because you are my father." The love which flows directly out of the connection is the most spontaneous, the most natural, and the most fresh of all.

And who is there among us who may not this moment yield this love to Almighty God, if with simple, unsophisticated mind, like those listeners who clustered round the feet of Our Lord on the verdant lily-clad hill where He delivered His great Sermon, he will but open the ears of his heart to those great and glorious illustrations of God's Fatherhood, which Heaven's great Ambassador proposes: "Behold the fowls of the air, for they sow not, neither do they reap, nor gather into barns; yet your Heavenly Father feedeth them. Are ye not much better than they?"

. . . "Therefore take no thought, saying, What shall we eat? or, What shall we drink? or, Wherewithal shall we be clothed? (for after all these things do the Gentiles seek:) *for your Heavenly Father knoweth that ye need all these things.*" . . . "What man is there of you, whom if his son ask bread, will he give him a stone? or if he ask a fish, will he give him a serpent? If ye then, being evil, know how to give good gifts unto your children, how much more shall *your Father which is in heaven give good things to them that ask Him?*"

2. The next form of love which is developed in the life of the individual man is the love of gratitude. This, too, is felt, in the first instance, toward parents. The infant becomes a child, and, together with natural affection for its parents, the child soon begins to feel a sense of their kindness to him. He feels that no one wishes him well with the same heartiness and devotion as they; and because it is in our nature to be won by kindness, he responds to their love; and this is his earliest exercise of gratitude. It is important to observe, that what he is attracted by—what stirs in him the love of gratitude—is not so much the benefits received from the parent, as the mind of kindness which those benefits evince. For conceive the case (yet it wants no conceiving, it is often realized) of a stranger, cold in his manners and patronizing in his deportment, approaching a child with presents. The presents may be acceptable—just what the child would wish to possess—they may glitter with those bawbles which are so attractive to the childish mind, and the recipient may enter upon the possession and enjoyment of them; but in vain does the stranger at-

tempt to conciliate good-will in this manner. The child is shy of him, does not trust him—a sure sign that it does not love him. On the other hand, the parents of the child may be poor, and unable to make presents; but it matters not, as far as the gratitude felt for them is concerned. The child has such assurances of their deep and living interest in him, those assurances have been given so naturally, so unceasingly, so spontaneously, that it has a thorough confidence in their affection, and loves them again for their kindness, not for the manifestations of it.

Now, that this love of gratitude may be, is to be, ought to be, felt toward God, it needs not many words to prove. "We love Him," says St. John, "because He first loved us." Gratitude toward God is the one great moral engine which the Gospel makes use of in subduing the will and sanctifying the heart of man. What is the Gospel but a most astounding display of the Divine Mercy, by which God proposes to carry the fortress of the human heart, which stands out against all the artillery of His threatenings? It is a Revelation of Love to all mankind—Love of such fervor and intensity, that it moved God to make the only sacrifice He was capable of making, to give His Only-Begotten Son to be the propitiation for our sins. It is announced, that in the death of that Son all have died, have paid the penalty and endured the curse of sin, and that henceforth the curse is abolished for all who simply hold to Him by faith; that all such are not only justified by the righteousness of Christ, but secured and shielded by His living intercession. Now the response of the sinner's heart to this Love of God is the one great secret of sanctification. To open wide the windows of our hearts, and to allow the light of this Love to flood every dark chink and cranny of the soul, this it is to be sanctified. For as the moon shines, not by its own light, but by giving back the radiance which the sun sheds upon it, so our hearts can no otherwise shine in holiness than by giving back, in the exercise of adoring gratitude, the light of the Divine Love, as manifested to us in Jesus Christ; as it is written, "We love Him" (and the love of God is the sum and substance of holiness) "because He first loved us." Observe the accuracy of the expression: "We love Him"—not because He ransomed our souls, forgave us, gave us His Son, or conferred any other benefit upon us; but "because He first *loved* us." We must not represent gratitude as a sordid affection, responding only to what we *get* from God. It responds to the sentiment of the giver, not to the gift. What attracts us is the astonishing Love of our Heavenly Father, in the face of all our indesert, guilt, rebellion, vileness. What God gives, He gives because His Fatherly heart is set upon us. It is His parental tenderness, of which the Gospel is so illustrious a display, which conciliates our confidence, makes us trust Him, and deposit our cares and troubles in His ear.

3. The third form of love to which we rise in the order of Nature is the love of moral esteem. Arrived at years of discretion, the child yields to its parents a less instinctive and more deliberate affection than it has yet been capable of. It observes in them uprightness of purpose, consistency of their conduct with their professions, sincerity, kindness, and all the other elements of character which go to make up goodness.

He esteems and venerates them for the possession of these qualities. Other people seem to him shallow and insincere in comparison; his parents have a weight of character, which commands his respect.

Now this love of moral esteem is one of the chief and one of the highest forms which the love of God takes. And if we were required to draw any distinction between the words of our text, we should call the love of natural affection "love with the soul," the love of gratitude "love with the heart," and the love of moral esteem "love with the mind." We are to love God, not only because He is good *to us*, but because He is so lovable. And the amiability of God consists in His moral perfections, and in the harmony of these perfections, and their exact adjustment and relations. The beauty of light consists in such an adjustment of the various rays composing it (such a happy mixture between the sombre rays and the brighter rays) that light is a perfectly pure and transparent medium, enables us thoroughly to explore any object which is submitted to us, while, at the same time, it does not dazzle or pain the eye. If the dark rays too much preponderated, we could not see clearly; if there were an undue preponderance of the bright rays, we should be dazzled and blinded. Now God is said to be Light in Holy Scripture, and the great thought brought out by this image is, that two classes of moral perfections, Holiness on the one hand, and Love on the other, are in His character harmoniously blended together. In virtue of God's holiness, or abhorrence of evil, there is an awfulness about His character which banishes from Him the wilful sinner, while in the reconciled sinner it stirs an emotion not of slavish fear, but of profound abasement. While in virtue of God's boundless Love (including under that term His Mercy and Compassion, as well as His Bounty and Benevolence) there is an attractiveness about His character which is calculated to win the heart of man even in the state of deepest moral degradation. We know that these opposite perfections are harmonized in the work of Christ; that in the Cross of His Son God is most illustriously seen, expressing at once the deepest abhorrence of sin and the most intense love for the sinner. But it is more to our present purpose to remark how the various attributes of God are reflected in the Humanity of Christ, who is, as St. Paul tells us, the express Image of God's Person. Moral esteem for Christ's character is in truth moral esteem for God's character. Should we then, let us ask ourselves, by way of ascertaining our love for God, have been really attracted by a character such as Christ's is represented to have been? Should we have been drawn insensibly into the circle of His influence, as the disciples were, by the words of grace which hung upon His lips, by the felt unearthliness which His Presence and demeanor shed around Him? Should we have admired the sterner as well as the softer side of His character—His fulminations against hypocrisy as well as His tender solicitude for, and sympathy with, the fallen? This love of moral esteem toward Christ was the salient feature in the religious character of the late Dr. Arnold, the one thought which colored all his sentiments of devotion. It requires some stamina of character to feel this moral esteem for any one. The love which arises from natural affection, from gratitude, from sympathy in trouble, from a mere fancy which can give no account of itself, is much more common in the world than the love of moral esteem. In order to esteem worth, there must be worth in him who is to show the esteem. And it asks more than mere worth, it asks a large measure of grace, to appreciate the extraordinary beauty and excellence of Our Blessed Lord's character, and to respond to it (as the devout man above alluded to responded) with profound, adoring veneration.

4. There is yet another kind of love which I must mention, because it is a clearly distinct sentiment from any of those which we have hitherto reviewed. It is the love of benevolence—the feeling which prompts us to wish good to others, and, as far as in us lies, to do it. A moment's consideration will serve to show that this is altogether distinct from the love of moral esteem. God loves the sinner, even when lying in his sins, with the love of benevolence. This Love of Benevolence on God's part is the source whence flowed to a guilty world the blessings of Redemption. "God commendeth His Love toward us," we are told, "in that, while we were yet sinners, Christ died for us." But it cannot be supposed that God has for sinners any love of moral esteem. He who is of purer eyes than to behold iniquity cannot regard iniquity with complacency. God's moral estimate of a world lost in sin, even while He had it at heart to save them by the Sacrifice of His Son, is thus painted by the Psalmist: "God looked down from Heaven upon the children of men, to see if there were any that would understand, and seek after God. But they are all gone out of the way, they are altogether become abominable; there

is also none that doeth good, no not one." And it is clear that among men also a feeling of benevolence toward miserable and degraded fellow-creatures may find place, even where there is (and can be) no feeling at all of moral esteem. A good man may strive with great earnestness to restore one who has lost his character, and to reinstate him in the position from which he has fallen, while the very fact of the object of this kindness having lost character precludes all esteem for the present. Then the question arises, whether this love of benevolence can be exercised toward God? Surely it may. It has been defined as the love which prompts good wishes and endeavors on behalf of another. Now ought not our hearts to be fondly set upon, and our endeavors directed toward, God's glory? Should we not long to further the interests of Christ by every means in our power? Should we not eagerly push in, wherever there is an opening, to promote His cause? Alas! it is not a question; there can be no doubt that this spirit should animate us all; there can be no doubt that by this spirit we all profess to be animated, as often as we pray, "Hallowed be Thy Name. Thy kingdom come. Thy will be done in earth, as it is in Heaven." But putting aside our professions, what is the real state of the case as regards our hearts? How many of us can honestly say that our most fervent wishes are embarked in the cause of Christ? There is plenty of room, God knows, for the advancement of that cause. There are souls steeped in misery, ignorance, and sin, all around us. There are good enterprises on foot by the hundred, which may be furthered by our money, or, if we have not money to spend, by an expenditure of time and labor. There are heathens abroad, waiting to be converted; and there are baptized heathens at home, waiting to be instructed in their privileges, and taught their high vocation. Now, are we occupying to the best of our ability any single corner of this vast field of usefulness? Have we ever seriously said to ourselves, "I wish to do something for my Lord and in His interests before I die—I wish to push His cause forward in my generation with all the energy I can muster?" To say this seriously is to exercise toward God, and Christ who is God, the love of benevolence. And, until we can in some measure say it seriously, we cannot say our Lord's Prayer quite sincerely; for this prayer assuredly implies that God's interests are nearer to the petitioner's heart than the supply of his own wants. Oh, this Lord's Prayer, what a canon does it supply for testing and correcting our spiritual state! How surely and infallibly does conformity to the spirit of it imply growth in grace! Therefore, Lord, conform us more and more to its spirit, and

"Teach us this, and every day,
To live more nearly as we pray."

CHAPTER VIII.

OF THE AFFINITY BETWEEN GOD AND MAN, IN REGARD OF MAN'S WANTS AND GOD'S FULNESS.

"*In the last day, that great day of the feast, Jesus stood and cried, saying, If any man thirst, let him come unto Me, and drink. He that believeth on Me, as the Scripture hath said, out of his belly shall flow rivers of living water.*" . . . . "*Many of the people therefore, when they heard this saying, said, Of a truth this is the Prophet. Others said, This is the Christ.*"—JOHN vii. 37, 38, 40, 41.

THE above weighty saying of Our Blessed Lord produced among some of His hearers an immediate conviction that He was the Prophet whom the Jews looked for—that he was the Christ. We gather from hence that these words meet some instinct of the human heart; that Our Lord, when uttering them, struck a note which vibrated in the inmost souls of His hearers. Now, what shall we suppose to have been the secret of their effect?

It was no doubt this, that many of the audience (all those of them, probably, in whom there was any seriousness or thoughtfulness of character) felt that they themselves were in a spiritual sense athirst, that there was a craving in the inner man after light, and truth, and love, which nothing upon earth met. When, therefore, the very remarkable Personage, who had recently appeared in their midst, stood forth and said, "If any man thirst, let him come unto Me, and drink," they felt that He was making an offer, of which they had need to avail themselves, that His word interpreted the longing of their souls, and held out a hope of satisfying it. They are convinced of His claims, by His offering them exactly what they had felt the want of.

We have been led, in the course of the argument of this work, to the subject of the love of God; and we begin by observing that, in order to the existence of love between two parties, there must be a secret affinity between them, in virtue of which one supplies what the other needs. This is visible in all the forms of human friendship. Friendship by no means seems to take root most deeply between persons of similar characters and sentiments. Rather the contrary as a general rule. Friendship is not a monotony, in which each of the characters sounds forth the same note; but a harmony, in which two notes are combined, which have some relation immediately recognized by the ear. Thus it is, to take the most obvious instance, in the case of friendship between the sexes, to which the name of love is commonly appropriated. The general foundation of that affection is just this, that one sex supplies those elements of character and feeling which the other lacks, the man being formed for activity, enterprise, labor, and to meet the brunt of life; the woman for endurance, tenderness, and domestic duties. It is not, of course, dissimilarity alone which constitutes the tie (dissimilarity, *if the dissimilars be not related to one another*, is only another name for discord), but dissimilarity of such a kind as to make one sex the complement and helpmate of the other. The man needs sympathy and confidential friendship, which the woman supplies; the woman in her turn needs support, protection, counsel, which it is the man's part to furnish. And thus, to accommodate to our purpose the words of the Apostle on a different subject, the abundance of the one is a supply for the want of the other, that the other's abundance also may be a supply for his want. In short, the principle which brings persons together in human friendship resembles the principle which lies at the foundation of commercial intercourse. A. produces what B. wants; and B. in his turn produces what A. wants. This mutual want of one another's productions draws together A. and B., and inclines them to exchange commodities, and to live near one another in mutual interdependence. Well; it is the same with character as with commodities. The characters of all want some element which the character of some other might supply. When we find that other, and are drawn toward him by an instinct which assures us that his disposition and qualities are the complement of our own—the attraction is called friendship or love, according as it subsists between persons of the same or of different sexes. In either case the secret of the attraction is precisely the same.

We do not speak of friendship among material objects; but affinities are observable among these, which rest upon the same principle of mutual interdependence. We will take one of these analogies in the lower world, to illustrate our subject further. Trees, then, are fed by the air and light of heaven, much in the same way as our bodies are kept alive by appropriate sustenance. Exclude all light and air from a tree, shut it up in a close and dark chamber, and it will speedily wither. Bring it forth again into the fresh air and sunlight, and the pores of its leaves will drink in the nourishment congenial to them, and seem to revive. No two objects can be more dissimilar than the tree and the air—the one a solid trunk of wood, never shifting from its place, the other a most subtle and imperceptible fluid which every wind sets in motion. Yet there is a secret affinity between them, which makes them necessary to one another, by which the two hang together in the marvellous system of Nature. The air is charged with its gases, by which it stimulates and quickens vegetation. The plants, on the other hand, need the circulation of this fluid through their veins. The air bestows itself upon the plants for their nourishment. The plants, on the other hand, make a return to the air, in the shape of the perfumes which some of them exhale. This is one out of many instances of an affinity in Nature, by which things mutually supplement one another. It is on a similar affinity, higher up in the scale of creation, that what we call friendship or love is founded.

This being premised, we now observe that the fact of man's being required in the Holy Scriptures to love God, indicates an affinity between man and God, by which man stands in urgent need of God, and God, too, has need of man, for the manifestation of His infinite perfections.

1. First, man, though a poor child of earth, fast rooted in this low and filthy soil, has an urgent need of God in His nature, just as the tree has a need of

light and air. When this need makes itself felt in a man's consciousness, he then realizes the experience of the Psalmist: "My soul is athirst for God, yea, even for the living God." And he is then arrested by, and disposed to listen to, the offer made by the Son of God: "If any man thirst, let him come unto Me, and drink."

But let us trace man's need of God more particularly, and seek to understand in what it consists.

In a certain sense, of course, all things have need of God, in order to their continuance in being and in well-being. He is the Preserver as well as the Creator of all things, and upholds them (in the Person of the Son) by the word of His power. If the Heavenly Father ceased to work even for a moment, if His energy and the support of His arm were for a moment withdrawn, the colors would fade from the robe of Nature, and the lights of the firmament would be extinguished, and the waters of the earth would fail and dry up in their channels, and the whole fabric of the universe would collapse, as an arch falls to pieces when the keystone is withdrawn. God is not only the ground, but the momentary support, of all existence.

It is clear, however, that the need which man, as man, has of God must be something which distinguishes him from the inferior creation. Inanimate and irrational creatures never are, never could be, exhorted to love God; and those who, like men, are so exhorted, must have some special affinity to God, some special need of Him, in virtue of which the love of God becomes for them at once a possibility and duty.

In what, then, does this special affinity stand? Consider the craving of man after the Infinite, so that his understanding is never satisfied with the truth which it discovers, nor his appetite with the good that it finds in created existence.

(1) First his understanding is never satisfied with the truth which it contrives to reach. The present is an age of discovery. The secrets of Nature are more and more explored, and yield themselves up, one after another, to the scrutiny of man. Now, the point to which we call attention at present is the thirst of man after knowledge, to which this ceaseless scrutiny bears witness. It is true, indeed, that Arts are founded upon the Sciences, and that most of the important discoveries which are made have some bearing upon our condition—tend to furnish human life with conveniences, comforts, and luxuries. But it is not only the desire of a more comfortable existence, of a better-furnished life, which stimulates the discovery. There is a nobler stimulus than this behind; the thirst for knowledge which is inbred in the human mind. There is nothing more deeply interesting to an intelligent man than discovery. It is as if God had proposed to us in Nature, in life, in our own hearts, certain enigmas, and had challenged human ingenuity to the solution of them, according to that word of King Solomon's: "It is the glory of God to conceal a thing: but the honor of kings is to search out a matter." But observe how, immediately upon a discovery being made, it loses its interest, and the vivid colors fade in which it was dressed while our minds were making it. Truth once established palls upon us; and we immediately go in quest of some fresh truth. It

would seem that just as the pleasure of hunting is not derived from the game which is caught, but from the exercise and excitement of the pursuit, so it is not truth which interests man, or at all events not the truth which he contrives to reach by his natural faculties, but only the quest of it. You see the restlessness of this quest in the pursuit of religious as well as of scientific truth. The inbred curiosity of the mind, which desires above all things to know, even where it is effectually precluded from knowledge, has ever been the fruitful source of heresies and fantastic speculations. Men eschew the plain preceptive parts of the Bible, and its more prominent doctrines, which have been sounded in their ears from childhood, and have now become to them like a popular air, which has had a long run, and has been sung at every concert, and hackneyed upon every street-organ, till it now haunts the hearer in his solitude ; the mind seeks something new, original, lively ; and works are written or theories broached to meet the demand—new views of unfulfilled Prophecy (which offers a vast field to the curious), speculations on the last times and our nearness to them, unhallowed attempts to divest religion of its mysteries, and to make it all plain and level to the understanding. All this is the natural instinct of the human mind to seek truth, running wild, and getting out of the groove which God has marked out for it to move in.

But shall we suppose that there is nothing corresponding to this restless thirst after knowledge in the human mind ? Is the mind to fret itself forever in the pursuit of truth, and never reach the goal of its desires? Is there no highest truth, in which the understanding may at length acquiesce? Not so. The Holy Scriptures say that God is Light; and again that He is the Father of lights. Again, they say that Christ is the Wisdom of God, and that in Him are hid all the treasures of wisdom and knowledge. When, therefore, man displays an insatiable desire to know, to read the riddle of Nature, the riddle of his own life, the riddle of his hereafter, he should remind himself that God Himself is the only satisfaction of this desire, that he has an intellect formed to receive the Light of God, a Light which one day will clear up all mysteries, whether of Nature, or of life, or of the future.

And this Light of God, my reader, you shall enjoy in a measure here below, not by any painful straining of the reason after truth, but by the entire submission of thy will to God's Will, and by the diligent purification of thy heart from all unruly passions. Desires and passions cloud the judgment, and shut out the clear, dry light of Truth.

(2) But, secondly, man craves after the Infinite Good, as well as after the Infinite Truth, and never finds it here below.

This craving after good is attested by the mischievous excesses of intemperance. What is the instinct which prompts man to intemperance in its various forms, which prompts him to invent new delicacies, new luxuries, and to stimulate the bodily appetite by all sorts of artificial means? That it is an instinct peculiar to him as man is clear. We find no intemperance among the lower creatures; they simply satisfy the natural appetite with the food which happens to be thrown in their way, but do not injure health by overfeeding, much less aim at increasing the deliciousness of the animal gratification by well-mixed bowls or highly-flavored condiments. The real account of intemperance is this, that man has not only an animal but a rational appetite to satisfy; by the constitution of his mind he thirsts after a good which he finds in no created object. The instinct, misdirected by the Fall, goes astray. Having a hungry spirit, he makes a desperate effort to extract from bodily enjoyments that which may appease its cravings. He imposes upon the body a double tax, to meet the demands of the spirit, if possible, as well as its own demands. But the body resembles a people in this respect; it is impoverished and enfeebled by undue and excessive taxation. It will meet the demands of its own animal appetites readily enough, and be none the worse for the payment; but the additional demands of the spirit's hunger it cannot bear. Accordingly, it breaks down under them. Premature decay is the almost certain consequence of intemperate excesses.

But there are more refined ways in which men endeavor to satisfy the craving of their immortal spirits after good. They seek admiration. The esteem of a little narrow circle in their immediate neighborhood; preëminence of whatever sort, whether of ability, or position, or of mere worldly wealth; the flattering speeches which are a sort of homage to superiority—how dear are these things to the soul! Not that the soul rests in them; having tasted them, it immediately craves for new enjoyments; it is after a wider reputation, a higher preëminence, a more refined and less palpable flattery. The *best* form of earthly good, with which the spirit seeks to satisfy its hunger, is that of human sympathy. It makes idols of the natural affections—plants for itself, as far as it can, a domestic and a social Paradise. The unfortunate point here is, that the trees of the Paradise, like Jonah's gourd, are apt to be smitten by the earthworm of death. And, independently of their being so smitten, we may certainly say that no mere natural affection can satisfy the craving of the human heart after love. Nothing is found on earth commensurate to that craving; no fellow-creature can fill the void. But the Creator can. Do we long after a joyous exhilaration of the spirit, which, as an exuberant mounting flood, shall tide us over the difficulties of our career? The Holy Spirit is the source of this inward joy, as it is written, "Be not drunk with wine, wherein is excess; but be filled with the Spirit." Do we thirst after esteem and admiration? Human esteem is but a taper: the real sunlight of the soul is the smile of God's approbation, making itself felt there. Is preëminence our aim? He is the Fountain of Honor; and the dignities of His Kingdom are bestowed on those who are least and lowest in their own esteem. Do we long, with an unquenchable longing, for sympathy? He is Love; and, in virtue of the Incarnation, He can be touched with the feeling of our infirmities; and death, so far from breaking off our intercourse with Him, admits us into His more immediate Presence, and cements that communion, which it is the joy and delight of renewed hearts to hold with Him here below.

Such, then, are man's two great wants, viewed as an immortal spirit—a want of the Infinite Truth, and the want of the Infinite Good, a want of Light and a want of Love. These wants are forever making themselves felt in the human consciousness in various forms. Man is like a noble tree planted in the earth, which can live only by drinking in the air and sunlight of Heaven. The Fall has walled him up in a dark enclosure of selfishness and sensuality; but, as he cannot live without light and warmth, he tries to expand his branches toward certain wretched tapers, which are burning in the interior. But they are never enough for him. Without the sun he cannot thrive. "His soul is athirst for God."

2. But we said that the ground of all love is the mutual dependence of the parties, between whom it subsists, on one another. Does God, then, in any sense depend upon man? Is man in any sense necessary to God? Necessary in this sense, only, as a field of display for the Divine Perfections. We are to conceive of God as an exuberant, full-charged Ocean of Truth, and Goodness, and Mercy, ready to pour itself over into the creatures, as receptacles of its fulness. God longs and loves to give, to communicate, to bless—it is the great feature of His perfection. He longs to surround Himself with intelligent, happy, joyous creatures, and to lavish upon them all the resources of His Infinite Goodness. And here we may catch a glimpse of the reason why evil was permitted. In the heart of God was a fund of mercy and tenderness, which, by the very perfection of His Nature, He longed to expend, but could find no scope for the exercise of it, except by the admission of evil into His universe. To be bounteous to creatures still retaining their integrity—oh! this is a very inadequate effect

of God's goodness. He can be bounteous, fatherly, infinitely loving, even to the unthankful. and the evil —to the vile, the degraded, the abominable; this is the great glory of His character, which the Gospel has unveiled and exposed to the gaze of poor fallen man. But mercy never could have poured itself forth, had there not been vessels of mercy to receive it. And vessels of *mercy* could never have existed, had there been no transgression—for righteous creatures need no mercy. We may certainly, therefore, recognize between God and man a natural reciprocity, which makes man necessary to God in something of the same sense as an object of charity is necessary to a liberal and large-hearted donor, deeply touched with the distresses of his fellow-men. Such a one cannot sit at home and lap himself in luxury; there is a sentiment of compassion in his heart, which drives him into the courts and alleys to seek out objects of relief. In like manner, God's fulness of compassion and bounty drives Him to the supply of man's necessities. He is the only Being who *can* satisfy those deep wants of the soul. And from His intrinsic goodness He longs to satisfy them.

My readers, have you been ever brought, by reflection upon your own experience, to the conclusion that your immortal spirit cannot be satisfied by any contentment which earth has to offer? Then, when God is announced to you as Light and Love, you cannot but see a suitability in the message, which commends it to your reason; your heart cannot but give back an echo, when this view of God first dawns on your apprehension, as the chords of Memnon's statue gave forth a musical sound, when it was smitten with the early sunbeam. It was no doubt an experience of this kind which many of the people went through, when Our Lord uttered in their hearing that sublime invitation: "If any man thirst, let him come unto Me, and drink." They were conscious of a thirst in the depths of their spirit; and He who offered thus solemnly to quench it must be God's Ambassador, charged with a message for them—must be the Prophet and the Christ indeed.—But an ambassador only! Surely He claims a prerogative beyond this. Let us hear Him again. "If any man thirst, let him come" (not unto My Father, but) "unto *Me*, and drink." He Himself it is, who undertakes to quench the soul's deep thirst for Light and Love. Can he be less than the Infinite? If we could suppose Him for a moment to be less, would not His words be an arrogant blasphemy? Most clear it is that He who speaks thus is God over all blessed forever. And if you will come to Him, my reader, laying aside utterly all self-righteousness and all self-will, you shall know by experiment that the large pretensions which He here makes are no vain boasts. He shall give you the water whereof whosoever drinketh shall never thirst; and it shall be in you "a well of water, springing up into everlasting life."

CHAPTER IX.

OF THE FILIAL RELATION OF MAN TO GOD, UPON WHICH THE LOVE OF GOD IS FOUNDED.

"*God said, Let us make man in our image, after our likeness.*"—GEN. i. 26.

IT was man's prerogative, alone of all the creatures, to be made "in God's image, after God's likeness." This image and likeness man possesses in virtue of his being a son of God—a name which is never given to the lower creatures. There is always a likeness (either in feature, or in mind, or in both) between parents and children, which is the result of the child's being drawn out of the parents, and, being, in fact, a part of them. And what is the cause of the likeness of all men one to another—their likeness in the leading sentiments and affections of their nature, which the wise man touches upon, when he says, "As in water face answereth to face, so the heart of man to man?" Is it not this, that we had all "one father" originally; are all drawn out of Adam by natural generation? Hence it is that heart beats responsive to heart in every clime, and that such poets as Shakespeare and Burns, who portray human passions in the fresh, simple colors of Nature, are appreciated not only in this country, but wherever their language is understood. The likeness follows in the train of a brotherhood, or, which is the same thing, of a common fatherhood.

We traced in our last Chapter the correspondence between God and man, in regard to man's cravings after the Infinite Truth and the Infinite Good, and God's fulness. We saw that God, being both Light and Love, is the only object suited to man's needs and desires. We now trace an affinity of a different character subsisting between these two parties, in regard of man's special likeness to God, which is the result of his filial relation. It is because man is a son of God, although a lost and a prodigal son, that he is capable of loving Him, and is exhorted to do so. Let us notice the resemblances to God which still linger in fallen Human Nature, and prove this sonship.

Man, then, resembles God in the constitution of his nature and in his natural powers.

1. *In the constitution of his nature.*—It is well known that the word *us* in the fiat for the creation of man ("Let *us* make man in *our* image, after *our* likeness") refers to the plurality of Persons in the Godhead. Man is to be made, therefore, according to the words of this fiat, in the Image of the Trinity in Unity. If you look into the constitution of his nature, you may expect to find there a three in one, and a one in three. And this is what you do find. Holy Scripture teaches us that there are three (not two) elements in Human Nature, "body, soul, and spirit." St. Paul recognizes the three in that prayer of his for his Thessalonian converts: "Now the very God of peace sanctify you wholly; and I pray God your whole *spirit*

and soul and body be preserved blameless unto the coming of our Lord Jesus Christ." The distinction between these three elements of our nature is very clear, and generally admitted. By "the body" is to be understood the mass of matter which we carry about with us, with all the various animal properties that belong to it. Hunger and thirst are appetites of the body; nourishment and growth are processes which take place in it. Observe, too, that the body is the organ of the will, and the exponent of the character. When a man acts or speaks, his will sets his body in motion. And it is usually thought that, in his physiognomy and general appearance, there is something which betokens his disposition. By "the soul" we understand what, in our modern phrase, is more commonly called "the mind."[1] It is the mind which draws lessons from experience or from the senses, which reasons, thinks, forms conclusions from facts submitted to it. He who works a mathematical or geometrical problem works it with his mind, with the purely intellectual element of his nature; it must be quite clear that neither the body nor the religious faculty has any share whatsoever in the operation. By "the spirit," in Scripture phraseology, is to be understood that faculty by which man holds communion

[1] It is quite possible that I have not drawn correctly the distinction between "soul" and "spirit." But suffice it that my distinction is a palpable one. Even if incorrect, it does not invalidate the argument. Man's nature is, according to the Apostle, tripartite, however you explain the threefold division; and in other passages a very sharp distinction is drawn between "the soul" and "the spirit." This tripartite nature is a vestige in him of the Image of God, in Whose Nature there is a Trinity in Unity.

with God. The religious instinct, which prompts him, in the blindness of his natural heart, to worship any thing which presents itself as beneficial or wonderful —sun, moon, and stars, or even the cunningly-wrought works of his own hands—and which, under the guidance of Revelation, drives him to the throne of grace, and makes him pant after God as the hart after the water-brooks; this is that faculty which goes under the name of "the spirit." When a man prays (really and sincerely), he prays with the spirit, according to those words of the Apostle: "I will pray with the spirit, and I will pray with the understanding also." Now, the distinction of these three processes, hungering, reasoning, praying, must be obvious to all. Yet it is one and the same man who embraces them all in the unity of his own consciousness, who may say of himself at different periods, I hungered, I reasoned, I prayed. And it is true. The same being who receives food at one time, at another lifts up his soul to God, at another works the problem. Here, then, you find in the nature of man, the son of God, a constitution which shadows forth, so far as earthly things can shadow forth heavenly, the nature of the Most High. We are told that we may not confound the Persons in the Blessed Trinity; that the Father, the Son, and the Holy Spirit, are distinct—as distinct as the spirit is from the soul, and the soul from the body. Moreover, we read in Holy Scripture that God created all things by Jesus Christ, using the Son as His instrument in the creation of the world; and that His Son is "the effulgence of His glory, and the express image of His Person." Similarly the body, as we have seen, is the organ by which the will of man acts, and the exponent of his character. Moreover, in the Holy Trinity "we acknowledge each Person by Himself to be God and Lord," even as, in the human trinity, we call the spirit the man, the soul the man, the body the man, indifferently. Yet, notwithstanding their distinction, they are not three Gods, but one God; just as it is not a different, but the same man, who is conscious now of hungering, now of reasoning, now of praying. There is indeed a great and unfathomable mystery in the doctrine of the Holy Trinity, or (in other words) in the constitution of the Divine Nature, which we must receive without for a moment attempting to fathom it. But while we find in the constitution of our own nature a mystery equally insoluble, who shall cavil at this requirement? While I find in myself an intellectual being, a religious being, and a being the subject of animal appetites, and yet know that each of these beings is my own true self, and that all are bound up in the unity of one consciousness, shall I not put my hand upon my mouth, and lay my mouth in the dust, when God requires me to believe something of the same kind (at all events not more mysterious) respecting His Infinite Nature? And shall I not recognize in man, made in the image and after the likeness of God, the signature of the Triune Jehovah, and bless the condescension and grace of Him, who hath made us sons, to shadow forth His lineaments upon earth, and to love Him as only those who are sons can be required to love?

2. But, secondly, man resembles God *in his natural powers, both intellectual and moral.*

a. As regards his intellectual powers, consider that man is, like God, a creator. Works of Art, whether useful or ornamental, are, and are often called, creations. How manifold are the new discoveries, the new inventions, which man draws forth, year after year, from his creative genius—the time-piece, the microscope, the steamship, the steam-carriage, the sun-picture, the electric telegraph! All these things originally lay wrapped up in the human brain, and are its offspring. Look at the whole fabric of civilization, which is built up by the several arts. What a creation is it, how curious, how varied, how wonderful in all its districts! Just as God has His Universe, in which are mirrored the eternal, archetypal Ideas of the Divine Mind, so this civilization is Man's universe, the aggregate product of his intelligence and activity. It may possibly suggest itself here that some of the lower animals are producers no less than man. And so they are, in virtue of the instinct with which the Almighty has endowed them. The bird is the artisan of her nest, the bee of his cell, the beaver of his hut. But they are artisans only, working by a rule furnished to them, not architects, designing out of their own mental resources. They are producers only, not creators; they never make a variation, in the way of improvement, on foregone productions; and we argue conclusively that because they *do* never make it, they *can* never make it. Instinct dictates to them, as they work, "line upon line, precept upon precept;" but there is no single instance of their rising above this level—of their speculating upon an original design, and contriving the means whereby it may be carried into effect. But the creative faculty of man is still more evident in the ornamental arts, because here, more obviously than in the useful, man works according to no preconceived method or imposed condition, but throws out of his brain that which is new and original. A new melody, a new drama, a new picture, a new poem, are they not all (some more, some less, in proportion to the originality of the conception which is in them) creations? Is not this the very meaning of the word "*poem*," in the language from which it is drawn—a thing made, a piece of workmanship? So that, in respect of the rich and varied developments of the human mind in the different forms of Art, we need not hesitate to call man a creator. And this is the first aspect under which God is presented to us in Holy Scripture: "In the beginning God CREATED the heaven and the earth."

b. Then as to moral powers. The free-will of man, involving, as it does, a reason which is capable of balancing the grounds of a moral choice, a reason which can look into the future, and set an eternal recompense over against present pain—this will, which nothing can compel into obedience without destroying its nature; this will, which is capable of an intelligent, a princely, and a generous obedience, the grounds of which it understands, and the reasons of which it inwardly affirms; this will, which not only is capable of moving in accordance with the Law, but which, while it does so, echoes from its inmost depths that "the Law is holy, and just, and good"—this free-will is unquestionably a strong feature of the mind of our Heavenly Father, communicated to us His rational children. For He, too, directs all His actions "according to *the counsel* of His own will"—with a perfect and wise foresight of results. His will, indeed, most unlike ours, is ever in harmony with the eternal Rule of Right and Truth. Yet he is laid under no constraint, He is impelled by no necessity; but His will is ceaselessly influenced by the spontaneous, generous emotions of an Infinite Love.

And here a word may be usefully said, bearing upon our mode of acquitting ourselves in the hour of temptation. Some divines, by way of exalting the grace of God, are apt to throw into the shade the free-will of man; and, so long as the case of the obedient is alone contemplated, the teaching of such divines has, at all events, a specious appearance, and may defend itself by alleging a righteous horror of attributing too much to the efforts of man. But, when we come to the case of the disobedient, what is the tendency of views which detract from the freedom of the human will? Is it not to make the sin excusable? to represent the force of passion as having been equivalent to compulsion, and our own unwillingness to make a stand as having been inability? And has no thought of this kind ever crossed us at the very moment when it most behooved such thoughts to be absent—in the balancings of the mind, before we have consciously yielded to a temptation? Have we never, at that time, gladly entertained the suspicion, "Well, I am hardly a free agent; for this strong current of corrupt desire virtually lays a necessity upon me?" And would it not have been better, and might it not have been blessed to our deliverance in that hour, if we had considered the original nobleness of our own nature, in virtue of the free, independent, self-determining will with which the Creator has endowed us? Let us be assured that, in asserting the supremacy of this will against present enjoyment or immediate advantage, lies our true dignity, and that the Image of God cannot otherwise be restored in us fallen creatures than by the will's recognizing its own perfect freedom, and spurning away from it the allurements of sense and of the world.

Thus we have traced the resemblance of man to God in respect both of the constitution of his nature and of his natural faculties. This resemblance, as I have before remarked, is the effect of the filial relation in which man, as man, stands to God. I say man, *as man*, because it is quite obvious that the resemblances we have traced are to be found equally in every member of the human family, whether Christian or heathen, whether engrafted into the Church or beyond her pale. All have the threefold element —body, soul, and spirit—in their nature; all have a mind which is potentially (if not actually) creative; all alike are endowed with free-will, and the power of moral choice. And here a difficulty may arise in some minds, which seems to lie in the way of what has been said. Are we not told, it may be asked, that "we are the children of God *by faith in Christ Jesus?*" Do we not instruct our children that *in Baptism* "they are made members of Christ, children of God, and inheritors of the Kingdom of Heaven?" And how is this consistent with our being children originally, before the reception of Baptism, before the exercise of faith? The answer is very simple. Man, though a son of God in virtue of the original platform of his nature, has by sin turned his back upon his home, and, thus moving His Father's holy indignation, has become "a child of wrath." This fall and forfeiture of all domestic privilege having taken place, God in mercy proposes to reconstitute His family, alienated from Him by sin, on a new basis. His own Son takes flesh, that He may be the Head of this family, makes ample atonement for the sins of every man, and merits by a life of perfect righteousness the acceptance of all. Then it is announced to the world that all have, by the admission of evil into their nature, forfeited their original position in the family of God, but that this position through grace is now again thrown open to all. The children of men are exhorted by belief and by Baptism to unite themselves to Him, in whom the family is reconstituted, and united to Him to become sons and heirs of God —the destiny for which man had been created, but to which he proved untrue. But the very call implies, if you consider it closely, an affinity with God on the part of the persons called—an affinity overlaid (it may be) with sin, and ignorance, and error, but still subsisting in the groundwork of their nature. They are called to the fruition and enjoyment of God—as the Scriptures express it, "to His kingdom and glory." Can any one be called to this enjoyment who has no capacity for it? Could a stone, or a vegetable, or an animal, be called to share God's kingdom? Then man must have a capacity for this high enjoyment. And what gives him this capacity? His having been made originally for the kingdom; his having been created for sonship. His nature, it is true, has become by the Fall a ruin, an unsightly heap of rubbish, in which venomous reptiles lodge, and which is foul with the greenness of decay; but it is no less true that, when the rubbish is swept away, you may find in that nature the ground-plan of the Divine Image. We are not now speaking of the moral or spiritual attainments of our Nature, *but of its constitution and capabilities.*

Reader, one of the earliest steps toward the love of God is to meditate often and deeply on His Fatherhood, and on the filial relation in which we stand to Him. This of itself is sufficient to stir in the heart an emotion of love toward Him, and a desire (oh, if we had but strength to bring it to good effect!) to return from our wanderings, and to find a home and a rest in His Bosom. But if such be the effect of thinking of the bare relationship which subsists between God and us, how powerfully must such an effect be seconded by taking into account the manner in which God has proved His strong paternal feeling for us! If He is simply announced to us as the Father of our spirits, our hearts respond. But when He is presented to us as the Gospel presents Him—when we are assured that his Love was so true, so clinging, that even when we were in the depths of our degradation and ruin, fighting against Him with all the force of our will, He gave His only begotten Son to be the propitiation for our sins, parted with Him for a time, that He might undergo for us a death of most cruel pain and shame; then indeed the sentiment of love to Him becomes something more than a sentiment, begins to claim for itself a supremacy over the will, and to establish itself as a principle of action. God grant it may be so with you and me! It is a poor and cheap thing to hear of the Love of God (and a poorer and cheaper to speak of it) without a heart in some measure kindled, or at least longing to be kindled thereby. Pray we, therefore, with our Church: "O God, who hast prepared for them that love Thee such good things as pass man's understanding; pour into our hearts such love toward Thee, that we, loving Thee above all things, may obtain Thy promises, which exceed all that we can desire; through Jesus Christ our Lord. Amen."

CHAPTER X.

OF THE WAY IN WHICH GOD HAS MADE THE PRECEPT OF DIVINE LOVE PRACTICABLE TO US BY THE INCARNATION.

"*He that hath seen Me hath seen the Father.*"—JOHN xiv. 9.

IT has been shown in the preceding Chapters that God's infinite fulness corresponds to man's deep wants, and that man stands to God in the relationship of a son to a father. Whenever God is truly represented to man, this correspondence, this relationship, subsisting still in the groundwork of human nature, though covered and hidden by the rubbish of sinful and worldly lusts, wakens up an echo from the heart—an echo which says, however confusedly and indistinctly, "Verily, Thou art my Father."

It must be admitted, however, that this echo, the result of the correspondence and relationship aforesaid, is of itself and by itself more of a sentiment than of a principle. Let us understand the difference. A sentiment is a right and pure feeling on a moral or religious subject, which does not (or rather need not) go beyond feeling, which need not determine the will, or exert any decided influence over the character. Right sentiments make a man more amiable, without necessarily making him a better man. They render him an object of complacency, and perhaps of compassion, while they do not necessarily reform him. A principle, on the other hand, if it have something less of tenderness and of poetry, has more hardness of resolve than a sentiment, has a stronger element of the will in it. Now, it is quite clear that, if the love of God is to exert over us a practical influence (and, unless it does this, it certainly can be of no avail in the matter of our salvation), it must become a settled principle of character within us. A fine and generous emotion, if it be nothing more than emotion, how will it ever struggle with the manifold corruptions of a heart "deceitful above all things, and desperately wicked?" how will it ever renew a nature which, in its first germ and rudiment, is depraved, a nature "shapen in wickedness and conceived in sin?" Such emotion would be as if a little tongue of earthly flame had been applied to Elijah's sacrifice, after it had been steeped in water three times. The flame might have played for a moment on the victim and the wood, but, finding every material soaked, upon which it could naturally kindle, would have collapsed; would never have prevailed, as did God's lightning from heaven, against "the wood, and the stones, and the dust," or have "licked up the water that was in the trench."

The powerlessness of the love of God, considered as a mere sentiment, consists very mainly in the indefiniteness of the Object of love. "No man hath seen God at any time." It is not merely that we have not seen Him with our bodily eyes, it is not merely that an image of Jehovah was never painted upon mortal retina; but no finite mind has (apart from

Christ) a definite conception of the Divine character. "God is Light," and "God is Love"—these are blessed and precious truths; but if these assurances stood alone, if no other exhibition of God had been made to us than what is conveyed in descriptions of this sort, there would have been room for the remark that Light and Love are mere abstractions, and abstractions are powerless over the character and will of man. Were it not for the exhibition which He has made of Himself in Christ, we could only conceive of God as of an aggregate of abstractions; that is to say, we draw a notion of goodness, mercy, justice, love, truth, holiness, from our own little sphere and our own limited experience, and to the sum total of these notions we give the name of God. Add to this that the idea, when we have formed it, however captivating it may be, is not free from contradictions, perplexities, and mysteries insoluble. To state one of these perplexities. If God is to become an object of attraction to the human heart, we must think of Him as endowed with affections and sympathies. But what does affection, what does sympathy mean, as it exists in the Divine Nature? We know not, nor in our present state can we know. On the one hand, we cannot imagine God to be the subject of those turbulent, restless, and disquieting emotions which we call passions; for this would be to represent Him to ourselves as imperfect, and to detract from His infinite blessedness. Yet we have no notion of passions and affections but such as is drawn from our own nature and experience; and thus we must either be content to think of God as moved by these (which we see clearly to be wrong), or must think of Him as passionless (which perhaps would be worse practically, even if more correct theoretically). For, according to the constitution of our nature, it would be impossible to fix our affections on a wooden God, touched by no sympathy, and susceptible of no emotion.—Again, in thinking of God, we are forming an idea of the Infinite; and the Infinite transcends all thought and baffles all conception. If we indulge in speculations on such a subject, we shall soon be dazzled and blinded, and forced to confess that "clouds and darkness are round about" the great Object which we investigate. In short, the perfections and nature of God are to the human understanding what the sun in his full meridian splendor is to the human eye. No eye can look upon the sun in his strength without being blinded. Excess of light would superinduce darkness. And the reason of man, as infirm in the world of ideas as the eye is in the world of matter, cannot gaze steadily upon God's perfections without being confounded; can only catch some rays of His light, as they come to us refracted through the earthly atmosphere which surrounds us. "No man hath seen God at any time." So that if God had never been made flesh, and dwelt among us, the sentiment of Divine love must have been the most uncertain, indefinite, and confused of sentiments, utterly unable to render an account of itself, and much more to establish a permanent empire in the soul.

But (blessed be His Name for having thus facilitated His love to us!) the Word of God—He who had already revealed the Infinite in the works of Creation—*did* take flesh, appeared upon earth in our nature, and was found in fashion as a man. And now observe the relation in which our nature stands to the

Divine in the mystery of the Holy Incarnation. It becomes a medium through which men may look upon God—look upon Him with their bodily eyes (the holy Apostles did so), look upon Him also with their understandings, and with the eyes of their affections. We should effectually defeat our own object, if, by way of gaining more knowledge on the subject of light, we should gaze on the sun in his strength. But we may gain a knowledge of sunlight indirectly. We may interpose a medium between the sun's rays and our eyes. The optical instrument called the prism explains to us the properties and constitution of light. So does the natural object called the rainbow. In the prism and in the rainbow we see light analyzed, broken up into its component elements; and we then understand and see (without any injury or straining to the eye) that light consists of several rays, some of a bright and some of a sombre hue, which rays are the source of all the fair colors wherewith the robe of Nature is decked. Now, the humanity of Our blessed Lord, a holy, harmless, undefiled humanity, conceived of the Holy Ghost, and born of the Virgin Mary, is to the perfections of the Divine Nature exactly what the transparent prism, and the pure raindrops, are to the sun—a medium of exhibition. In the humanity of our Lord we can study the character and perfections of the Most High, without presumption, and at the same time without mistake. He represents God to us, puts God before us, with a vividness and a definiteness, which we could never gain from any description, however graphic and however just. God is made in Christ, if I may so speak with reverence, level to our apprehensions and our sympathies. *Level to our apprehen-*

sions. The Infinite has taken a finite nature like our own, and a finite nature like our own we can easily conceive of. Here is no abstract idea of perfection, but an actual, breathing embodiment of it, One who lived, and toiled, and suffered, a real man among men, who encountered all sorts of characters and incidents, and in every such encounter demeaned Himself with an admirable wisdom, sanctity, and love. We are not left to hypothesis as to God's sentiments upon human life, its scenes, and the personages who act in them; we see God Himself an actor in these scenes, coming athwart these personages, and delivering Himself on each occasion in sentiments the very tones of which are unearthly. Here, too, you find (in the humanity of Our Lord) the reconciliation of the apparent contradictions between mercy and righteous wrath. On the one hand, no amount or measure of moral degradation shuts out a sinner from His sympathy, or checks for an instant the outflow of His Divine compassion. The robber, the outlaw, the harlot, the adulteress—He has no word of severity for them as such, so long as they take shame to themselves for the evil that is in them, and welcome the glad tidings which He brings to them of a Father's love and pity. But there is another and a severe side to His character, whenever He comes across a want of truth, a dissembling of convictions, a hypocritical make-believe of religion, an outward homage without the submission of the will. The hollowness of Pharisaism always draws forth from His lips one loud, reiterated, sustained "Woe!" Whence we gather the sentiments of God toward sin, and learn to adjust Divine severity with Divine goodness. The love of God freely embraces all, however low they have fallen, who willingly take up their position as sinners, caring little or nothing for the outpointed finger of human scorn. But want of truth in all its forms, insincerity, hypocrisy, parade and demonstration of religious feeling, in short, any sacrifice which men do to the opinion of their fellow-creatures, is offensive to Him in the highest degree, and incompatible with His friendship. Such are God's sentiments toward sin, as our Lord Jesus has expounded them.—And again, *God is in Christ level to our sympathies.* There were emotions in Our Lord's human heart sundry and manifold, emotions of compassion, warm friendship, patriotism, zeal, righteous indignation, which are to be regarded by us, in virtue of the union subsisting between His humanity and the Godhead, not merely as affections incidental to our nature, but as conveying and representing to us what there is in the heart of God. Divine affections must ever (as I have remarked) be an insoluble mystery to us; but this is certain, that there is in the Divine Nature something which corresponds to, and is represented by, passion and affection in ourselves—something which, looked at through the medium of humanity, *is* passion and affection. We need not fear to conceive of God as stirred by the same pure and holy emotions which stirred the heart of Our Lord. It is the nearest approach our finite minds can make to the absolute truth.

Thus, then, by means of the Incarnation, God has reduced Himself to the level of human apprehensions and human sympathies. He gives us in Christ a definite object, upon which all our sentiments of love, loyalty, veneration, affection, may fasten; yet without fear of idolatry, inasmuch as this object is Divine. To conceive of Christ is to conceive of God; and to love Christ is to love God; for he that hath seen Christ hath seen the Father. Oh, let us adore His infinite condescension, who not only lays down this as the first and great commandment of His law, "Thou shalt love the Lord thy God with all thy heart, and with all thy soul, and with all thy mind," and thus seeks to persuade the will into compliance not by menaces of authority, but by the amiable attractions of love; but who also, knowing Himself to be (in the perfection of His absolute Nature) above the reach of our capacities, has smoothed the way for the fulfilment of this commandment, and removed all difficulties out of our path, by presenting Himself to us in fashion as a man, and allowing us to love Him through the medium of One, who was a partaker at once of His nature and of ours.

It is true, indeed, that we individually have never looked upon Our Lord Jesus Christ, and cannot therefore form as lively a conception of Him as those first disciples, who companied with Him all the time that He went in and out among men. And it seems to be intimated in Holy Scripture that the difficulty (and therefore the praise) of believing in Him and loving Him is, under these circumstances, enhanced; that our position is one of some disadvantage compared with that of the earliest believers. In this direction look the words of Our Lord to St. Thomas: "Thomas, because thou hast seen Me, thou hast believed: blessed are they that have not seen, and yet have believed." And St. Peter speaks to those whom he is addressing, of Jesus Christ, "whom having *not seen*, ye love;"

the thought in the mind of the Apostle being probably this, "Your faith is stronger, and your love more commendable than mine, who *have* seen Him." And yet the advantages are surely not all on one side. There can be no doubt that the mere association with Our Lord, in the days when He was compassed with natural (though not with sinful) infirmity, though it might have furnished a more exact impression of Him, would not have been nearly so conducive to reverence of feeling as our present view of Him down the vista of the past. The hunger and the thirst, and the weariness, and the buffetings, and the slights, and the mockeries, and the cruel injuries, are to *our* faith no drawbacks; rather the glory which now enfolds His Sacred Person has absorbed into itself these traits of human infirmity, and made them glow with its own lustre. But when the disciples looked upon them, as they were actually passing, these things would be hinderances rather than helps to their forming a right estimate of His holy dignity.—Consider, moreover, to how great an extent the inestimable possession of the Holy Gospels compensates us for the loss of all actual intercourse with Our Lord; how, by furnishing to us these four pictures, Our Merciful Father has again smoothed the way for us to love His Son, and through His Son to love Him. Consider that we have in these Gospels the very image of Christ (Himself the Image of God) as it was projected upon the mind of the Jew, reared in Old Testament associations; upon the mind of the Roman[1], the prompt and energetic

[1] This is Dr. Da Costa's idea. I have not his book (on "the Four Gospels") at hand; but it is he who, in adverting to the resemblance of style, often observed upon, between St. Mark's

conqueror of the world; upon the mind of the Greek, who represented the world's literature and intelligence; and finally, upon the mind of one who, for his profound insight into the deep things of God, and specially into the relations of the Son to the Father, has been called by way of eminence St. John the Divine. Here, therefore, you have four photographs of Our Lord in different postures, and with the minor incidents of the picture differently grouped. Photographs I may well call them, much more truly than pictures; because in the photograph the sun is the great designer, and the work of the artist is simply to arrange the position of the subject, and to prepare and expose the materials to the light. Similarly, the holy Evangelists, in providing likenesses of Our Lord for His Church, arranged the great Subject each of them from his own point of view, and according to the impression which Christ left upon his own mind; but they did little else than this; the light from Heaven, the brilliant light of inspiration, streamed in upon the dark chamber of their apprehensions, and secured the accuracy of the portrait in every minute particular.

Then, since our Merciful God has made the love of Himself thus easy, first by giving us an express Image of Himself in the sinless humanity of Jesus, and secondly, by portraying this Image in the narratives of the four Evangelists, our part is to ask ourselves very seriously whether our hearts are drawn toward the likeness, which has thus been furnished to us. Do

Gospel and Cæsar's Commentaries, insinuates that Marcus may have been "the devout soldier of them which waited on" Cornelius "continuallv."

we love with an adoring love, with a love which more and more establishes its empire within us, the character of Christ as it is presented to us by the Evangelists? I say, *as it is presented to us by the Evangelists*, because I am persuaded that the object of homage with many Christians is a Christ of their own fancy, not the Christ of Scripture, that is, of history. They copy into their fancy picture all the mild, and gentle, and merciful features of the original; but the indignant repudiation of hypocrisy, the keen-edged censure of religious formalism, the stern exposure of all stickling for the letter while the spirit is disregarded, the distinct repudiation of the world's estimate of all subjects—blessedness, misery, sin, piety, God—the positive severity to characters wanting in truth and wanting in tenderness—in short, that whole side of the Lord's mind which armed against Him Pharisaic prejudice and exclusiveness, and aroused a malignant hatred against His Person, without parallel in the annals of our race, all this scarcely enters at all into the estimate of Christ's character which many of His professing followers form. But to love Christ must surely imply (as I shall insist upon more at large in another Chapter) a sympathy with His antipathies. If we in no measure detest falsehood and formalism as He did, if we in no measure repudiate, as He did, the world's estimate of spiritual subjects, surely there is every reason to doubt whether, instead of Him, we are not worshipping a creation of our own brain. Oh, it is easy to love God (or to imagine that we love Him) when He comes preaching peace to all who will receive it, and scattering blessings with lavish hand upon the sufferers of the human race; but when He beats down with His fulminations the old idols of prejudice, which have grown green in our hearts, unmasks our hypocrisies, and gives the lie to every single maxim and principle of worldly policy—how then? Search your heart, my reader; are you worshipping a fictitious Christ, or the true one?

Perhaps you may find that you are worshipping, not a Person at all, but a doctrine, or a little group of doctrines, selected from the mass according to your own prepossessions, or the bias of your own theological school. Christianity, according to your view, does not consist in the simple, trustful love of Jesus, moulding the character into conformity with His image; but in a resolute (and, it must be confessed, an occasionally bitter) adherence to certain blessed and precious doctrines announced by the Apostle Paul, for the comfort and edification of the people of God. Justification of free grace and by faith only, sanctification of God's elect through the Spirit, and their preservation through faith unto salvation—allegiance to these formularies of doctrine and denunciations of all who do not give them an equally prominent place with yourself, is what you are substituting for the first and great commandment, "Thou shalt love the Lord thy God with all thy heart, and with all thy soul, and with all thy mind." Oh! beware. We are justified, doubtless, by faith. *But the Scripture never says that we are justified by believing in the doctrine of justification by faith.* We are justified, doubtless, by faith. But it is simply because faith is the heart's first approach to Christ, who by His own merit heals all who apply to Him. The faith, if genuine, fastens not on any doctrine, but on the Person of the Saviour, and works the renovation of the character through the love of Him which it engenders. Have you the faith which makes you an adherent of Himself? and is it working by love? Do you study His character, as it is portrayed by the Evangelists, looking often and lovingly upon His picture, as we do upon the portraits of those we love? Is it your delight to be continually reminded of His Presence, and do you instinctively seek that Presence in the intervals of business and amusement, and among the trials of the day? And do you delight to feel that you are especially in His Presence, when two or three are gathered together to commemorate His dying Love in the holy mysteries of His own appointment? And is your constant gaze upon Him in His Providence, in His Word, and in His Sacraments, secretly working in you a resemblance to His purity, as it is said that the wild animals who live in very high latitudes become white by constantly looking on the waste of snow which lies around them? These are the questions by which to determine our love of the Saviour, and therefore our love of God, whose image He is. And this love is the very criterion of Christian character. For, as on the one hand it is said, "Grace be with all those who love Our Lord Jesus Christ in sincerity;" so on the other are we warned that the lack of this love entails a curse on the disciple who lacks it: "If any man love not the Lord Jesus Christ, let him be Anathema Maranatha."

CHAPTER XI.

OF THE LOVE OF GRATITUDE.

"*We love Him, because He first loved us.*"—1 JOHN iv. 19.

IT was pointed out in a former Chapter that one main form which the love of God assumes is the form of gratitude. The love of gratitude (or, as it might be termed, of reciprocity) will form the subject of the present Chapter.

The love of gratitude is a sense (poured forth into the heart, and filling every corner of it) of God's Love to us. Observe the terms of the definition. *A sense of God's Love*—not a feeling awakened by God's Love. The two expressions may seem to signify the same thing; but, when we come to examine them, we shall find that the first goes far beyond the second.

Gratitude, as it is felt by man toward man, is generally no more than a feeling (or sentiment) awakened by kindness. If a man does me a kindness at a considerable sacrifice to himself, this kindness produces in my mind a movement toward him, a disposition to think well of him, to like him, and (if I can) to requite him. If I have been heretofore cold toward him, his kindness makes me thaw; if I have hitherto taken no interest in him, his kindness quickens in me such an interest. So the sun, by its action upon the face of Nature, thaws the crust of ice which had formed over the water, and quickens the seed which lay dead and dormant in the bowels of the earth.

But gratitude, as felt toward God, consists merely in a sense of His Love. The sense of His Love is not only the cause, but the essence, of ours. It does not resemble the thawing of the ice and the quickening of the seed by the sun's rays, so much as the reflection of his light by the moon and planets. Consider the two images, and you will see the difference of the things illustrated. The thawing of the ice, and the quickening of the seed, are effects in Nature produced by the sun's rays—influences of the sun felt in Nature, and showing themselves in certain changes there. But what is moonlight? Moonlight is something more than an operation produced by the sun—it is actually sunlight reflected by the moon. It is called moonlight, not because it proceeds from the moon (which is an opaque body, having no light in itself), but because the moon (as also the planets do) intercepts it and gives it back. Similarly, the love of man toward God is not merely a sentiment engendered in the human heart by the Love of God toward man. It is actually "God's" own "love" (to use the Apostle's expression), "shed forth in our hearts by the Holy Ghost which is given unto us;" it is not man's love at all, if you trace it up to its source; but God's Love, intercepted and returned upon Him from a heart which has the capacity of reciprocating it. It does not take its rise in our own bosoms; we have no other property in it than that of simply reflecting and giving it back.

Now we shall view the subject for a few moments under this image, because it conveys many profitable lessons :

1. If our love to God be only His Love to us reflected from our hearts, it must be quite clear that the more we expose our hearts to His Love, the more truly shall we love Him.

It is sometimes apprehended that by a too full and free exhibition of the Divine Love we may encourage sinners in their evil courses, and make them careless and licentious. But what shall we say to such reasoning, if the very essence of man's love to God stands in the apprehension of God's Love to him? Can we ever effectually sap sin's power over the heart, without implanting there sincere love to God? And if sincere love to God be nothing else than God's Love shed forth into and reflected by the heart, are we likely to implant it by hiding God's Love in a corner, and shutting up the heart of man from the apprehension of it? What would be thought of a man, who, being possessed of some jewel, and desiring to exhibit its beauty, and to make it flash and sparkle, should carefully enclose it in its casket, and exclude it from the light of the sun? The light in which it must flash and sparkle is not its own light; and therefore such a course would effectually defeat the end. And if the dull spirit of man is to be made to burn and shine with love to God, it must be brought out into the full blaze of God's Love—the fuller the blaze, the stronger will be the reflected light. And, for those who possess the love of God, the great method of making any solid advance in it must be surely a continual opening of the heart toward God's

Love, with a yearning desire to know more of it, to be profoundly indoctrinated into its freedom and fulness. If we are conscious of having sinned, it will do nothing for our restoration, rather it will throw us back to a greater distance than that to which the sin has already removed us, to doubt God's Love in respect of that particular sin. To regard Him as our tender Father, yearning over us after and notwithstanding our fall, watching with deep solicitude for the earliest symptom of a better mind, nay, as already having given us forgiveness through the Blood and Righteousness of His Son, this is the only method of restoration. And the longer we delay the contact of the heart with the pardoning Love of God, the more time we waste, and the longer we obstruct our own recovery.

2. It must, I suppose, strike every one that, if our love to God be nothing more than God's Love to us, shed forth into our hearts and reflected back thence, there can be no sort of merit or desert in it. Of this grace of love it may be said, as is said by the Apostle of ministerial gifts, "What hast thou that thou didst not receive? Now if thou didst receive it, why dost thou glory as if thou hadst not received it?" If we are in the first instance *recipients* of the Love, which flows from us back into the Bosom of of God, is not all ground of boasting cut away? And if there be no merit in the love of God, there is no merit in any human virtue. For love embraces all the duties of the first Table, according to that word of Christ's: "Thou shalt love the Lord thy God with all thy heart, and with all thy soul, and with all thy mind. This is the first and great commandment."

And in regard to the duties of the second Table, they are implicitly wrapped up in the first; for the love of our neighbor is prescribed by God, and is part therefore of the love of God. Thus all duties, if traced up to their original ground, resolve themselves into the love of God, and are fulfilled by that love. No duties therefore can lay claim to any merit, since this chief and summary duty has none.

3. But, thirdly, our illustration suggests this question, What is it which prevents our so realizing God's Love to us as to love Him in return? And, when pursued, it answers the question which it suggests. What is it which might prevent the earth from reflecting the warm and golden rays which the sun throws upon it? The circumstance of part of its surface being turned away from the sun might of course do this. And we might compare such part of the earth's surface to the spiritual state of the heathen. They are plunged in the night of ignorance and error, because the revelation of God's Love has never been made to them; they have never had their hearts exposed to the action of it. But Christians, who have been made acquainted with God's Love by the revelations of the Gospel—what can it be which prevents *their* realizing it in an effectual manner, so as to give it back? Our illustration here again stands us in stead. The earth's surface may be exposed to the sun: nevertheless, if you build a hovel over a part of it, with no aperture for the light, you prevent that part from reflecting the sun's rays. Now, there is a certain hovel built over the hearts of all of us, screening us from the light and warmth of Divine Love, and called unbelief. All the knowledge of God's Love in the world, without

faith in it, will avail nothing to make us reciprocate it. We may feel certain that the Love of God has been manifested in a marvellous way toward the whole human race; that it has been poured out without stint upon mankind in general, and yet may not ourselves (by reason of unbelief) so feel it as to reciprocate it. Just so a man in a dark hovel might be conscious that the sun was shining gloriously outside, yet himself might not either be lightened or warmed thereby. And therefore St. John, describing the process which is necessary in order to our reciprocating the Love of God, says, "We have known and believed the Love which God hath to us." "Known"—this is the first step; and it distinguishes Christians from the heathen; the heathen have not "known" the Love of God, except so far as Nature may have served to some of them as a revelation of it. But the knowing it is not of itself sufficient; the Love must be "believed" also, in order to its being given back; this is the second stage; and it distinguishes the true from the merely nominal Christian. He who not only knows the Love of God, but believes in it, enters upon the experimental enjoyment of it, and immediately reciprocates it.

It being now clearly seen that faith is the spring of the love of gratitude, it remains to inquire how this faith is to be obtained.

Now, in obtaining it there are two great truths to be kept in sight and made the foundation and regulating principle of all our efforts. First, that it is the gift of God. "To you it is *given*," writes St. Paul, "in the behalf of Christ, ... to *believe* on Him." And again: salvation by faith (and if salvation by faith, then surely faith itself, which is the instrument of our appropriating salvation) is said distinctly to be the gift of God: "By grace are ye saved through faith; and that not of yourselves; *it is the gift of God.*" Secondly, that the exercise of faith is designed to be a moral criterion between man and man; and that those who have heard of Christ are morally responsible for not exercising faith in Him .

From these two truths flow the following practical advices:

1. The gift of faith is to be sought in earnest and persevering prayer. "Lord, help Thou mine unbelief," "Increase my faith," is to be the ceaseless importunate cry of our hearts. And we must confess ourselves before God, not only destitute of faith, but *incapable of attaining it by our own efforts.* And though we must be very earnest in this prayer, yet we must be content to abide God's time for answering it, remembering how often in the stubbornness of our perverse hearts we have turned a deaf ear to the solicitations of His grace, and have thus merited that *He* should turn a deaf ear to our cry.

2. We should observe, for our encouragement, that our importunity in prayer is itself an answer to our petitions. There cannot be earnest prayer without some amount of faith, though it may not be a faith fully formed or developed, nor may as yet fasten upon those truths which are the leading features of the Gospel. "He that cometh to God must believe that He is, and that He is a rewarder of them that diligently seek Him." Consider how thoroughly unformed a faith those characters in the Gospel must have had, who yet are commended for their faith, and carry away their cure (or the cure of their friends) as

the recompense of it. It can have been nothing more, generally speaking, than a persuasion of Christ's power and willingness to heal—in the case of the woman with the issue of blood, it seems to have been nothing more than the idea that it was worth while making an experiment, as it might be successful. It is well to remember that, as you may infer from smoke that there is fire somewhere, though it may be smouldering beneath superincumbent fuel, and not even a spark may be visible, so you may infer from prayer that there is faith somewhere in the heart, though it may be well-nigh smothered beneath the load of natural corruption and infirmity. And of Christ it is said, that He will not quench the smoking flax. Prayer is the smoke which goes up from a heart, in which the first spark of faith has been dimly kindled.

3. Together with prayer, other means of bringing about the desired effect must be diligently used.

The chief of these will be the making God's Love a definite subject of meditation. This Love is to be inferred from the great fact of His having given His Son for us, which must be constantly placed before the mind with an effort to realize it. Our familiarity with the fact, or rather with the words which express it, exceedingly blunts and deadens our apprehensions of it. We must strive against the influence of this familiarity. We must endeavor to lift our minds out of the groove of certain formularies, in which the truth has been from our childhood conveyed to us; and to front, not a verbal proposition, but the great reality itself. The great reality is, that God gave up for man, out of love to man, and for the salvation of man, the one thing in the Universe which could to God be a sacrifice. "God so loved the world, that He gave His Only-Begotten Son, that whosoever believeth in Him should not perish, but have everlasting life." "He gave His Son." We know the exceeding difficulty with which a parent is induced to tear himself away from an only child. If the child is to be parted with to adverse or doubtful fortunes, the struggle is more dreadful still. If an only son is to be sent to a war upon the losing side, where daily risks have to be run, daily hardships to be encountered, and a violent death is all but certain, some one strong absorbing passion must have got the mastery of the parent's heart, before he could be brought to consent to such a sacrifice. Now, this is the aspect under which God would have us think of His Love. His Son, of glory equal, of majesty coeternal with His own, had lain in His Bosom from all eternity, had been bound to Him in that closest of all unions, the unity of the Godhead. But God went forth in the longings of ardent parental affection to those *created* children of His, who had abandoned communion with Him, and in whom His Image (the image at least of His moral perfections) was altogether effaced. Not the smallest signs of a better mind did they give; every cry which reached Heaven from earth was a cry of defiance and hostility; but as the undutifulness of a son does not stifle the father's affection and anxiety to reclaim him, so the fall of man did not repress the tenderness of God's Love for him, but on the other hand called forth the most wonderful exercise of it. Rather than that His created children should perish eternally, God preferred making over His uncreated Son to hardship, and toil, and a bloody and shameful death on their behalf. That bloody and shameful death was in the counsels of His wisdom expiatory of sin; it was a satisfaction of the Divine justice; and it harmonized all the Divine perfections with the salvation of man. This, however, is not the point in it to which attention is now called. We are not speaking of the efficacy of the Sacrifice, but of the Love of God in providing the Sacrifice. It is of no small importance, as we have said in an earlier Chapter, to observe this distinction. "We love Him," says the Apostle—not because He has conferred a particular and high benefit upon us—not even because He has given His Son for us—but "because He first loved us." It is the Love of God which attracts our gratitude, not the benefit which, in the exercise of that Love, He hath conferred. The affections of the human heart cannot be constrained by benefits, independently of the mind of the benefactor. And therefore, if our hearts are to be given to God, the thing which we need first and before all other things is assurance of His sympathy. And of this He has vouchsafed to us the strongest and most irrefragable assurance in the gift of Christ. This gift we must strive to view, not only in its own intrinsic preciousness, as being the ransom of our souls, but in the Love which dictated it.

4. The last point which I shall mention for the obtaining of faith in God's Love, is *the acting as if we had it.* The ten lepers in the Gospel were bidden to go and show themselves to the priests, before they were cleansed. Now, the purpose of showing themselves to the priests was, that they might receive ceremonial purification, which the priests were directed not to confer unless they had first ascertained that

the leper was actually made whole. These lepers were instructed, then, to act upon an assumption, which was not yet realized; and in the acting upon it they found it realized; "it came to pass," we read, "that *as they went*, they were cleansed." Until, therefore, you obtain a lively faith and love, act as far as possible on the assumption that you have them. Endeavor to foment in your heart the poor faith and love which you at present have. Think much of God's Love as manifested, not only to mankind at large, but to yourself in particular. Express yourself toward Him in prayer *as if you loved Him*. Review His mercies in detail, and thank Him for them specifically. Praise Him with as much fervor as you at present are master of, in psalms, and hymns, and spiritual songs. "Aspire to God by brief but ardent ejaculations of your heart; admire His beauty; invoke His assistance, and cast yourself in spirit at the foot of His cross; adore His goodness; treat with Him often on the great concern of your salvation; give your soul to Him a thousand times a day; make a thousand different sorts of motions in your heart to excite you to a passionate and tender affection." [1] Stretch out your hand to Him as a child to a father, that He may conduct you; and while you are thus musing the fire shall kindle; your faith shall seem to burst through the superincumbent load of your natural corruption; and the Love of God, shed abroad in your heart by the Holy Ghost which is given you, shall return again into His Bosom, as rivers return into the great deep, whose full-charged fountains sent them forth.

[1] From the "Vie Dévote" of S. François de Sales.

CHAPTER XII.

OF THE LOVE OF GOD AS INVOLVING ANTIPATHY TO EVIL.

"*Ye that love the Lord, hate evil.*"—Ps. xcvii. 10.

"THE first of all the commandments is, Hear, O Israel: The Lord our God is one Lord: and thou shalt love the Lord thy God with all thy heart, and with all thy soul, and all thy mind, and with all thy strength."

Hence it is supremely important to ascertain how far we fulfil this commandment. And yet perhaps there is no point respecting our spiritual state which it is more hard to ascertain. There is no point on which the naturally deceitful heart is more apt to deceive us. And the reasons of this proneness to self-deceit upon a question so important are obvious. First, as the Apostle John says, "No man hath seen God at any time." And our ideas of that which we have never seen are necessarily undefined and vague. Mere description, however accurate, can never convey any thing fully. And, therefore, our very notion of God being vague, our obligation to love Him becomes somewhat vague also. And it contributes to this indefiniteness of impression that God is really so much above us—that there are in Him so many things strange to our experience and understanding, that "His thoughts are not our thoughts, neither are our ways His ways."

Now, an admirable practical test of the love of God is suggested in the passage which stands at the head of this Chapter, and shall form the subject of it. If we know comparatively little about God, if we find it hard to raise our understandings to the apprehension of His perfections, if, when we try to fix our thoughts upon Him, "clouds and darkness" are apt to gather round the mind—there is at least one subject with which we are thoroughly conversant from our youth upward, which presents itself in a thousand definite shapes, and by our dispositions toward which we may judge with tolerable certainty of our disposition toward God. That subject is evil—moral evil—in one word, sin. Who does not know what evil means? If I were to define it, I should fall into the logical error of making a definition more obscure than the thing defined. Evil is *with* us all day long, in our hearts—*around* us all day long, in our society. Our moral constitutions take it in continually, just as our bodies take in the air we breathe. As says the Christian poet—

"Sin is with man at morning break,
And through the livelong day,
Deafens the ear that fain would wake
To Nature's simple lay."

Now, of thus much respecting Almighty God we may be absolutely certain, that evil is His opposite. "God is light; and in Him is no darkness at all." We know what contradictories in reasoning are; they are two statements, which cannot possibly be both true or both false at the same time; the truth of one of them infers necessarily the falsehood of the other. We know what contradictories in nature are. Water destroys fire. Light expels darkness. Alkalies neutralize acids. The two cannot subsist together. Now, God (whatever else He may be) is the contradictory of evil. Evil stands in opposition to God. God lays His ban upon it, condemns it, forbids it, will in time demolish it utterly. What follows? That, if we hate evil, we must love God, even as, if we dread and dislike the darkness, we must welcome and long for the light. The two things infer one another, and there is no alternative. For, though the Psalmist in the exhortation, "O ye that love the Lord, see that ye hate the thing which is evil," seems at first sight to imply that they who love the Lord might possibly be slack in hating evil, the words are surely to be understood as a caution addressed to those who profess to love the Lord, having, indeed, a sense very similar to that motto upon God's foundation, which is recited by the Apostle Paul: "Let every one that nameth the name of Christ depart from iniquity."

By way, then, of testing the affections of our own hearts toward God, let us ascertain how we are disposed toward His opposite—evil. And, in order that we may do this the more easily, let us consider what is involved in the term, a hatred of evil.

It is clear, then, that to *hate* evil is something far more than merely to *shun*, or *avoid* it; that it is possible to avoid without hating it; nay, that not only is it possible, but that this is a phenomenon which not unfrequently meets us—of which, possibly, we have experience in ourselves. There are certain forms of sin to which all persons of strong passions and warm temperaments are naturally propense. Experience, or dread of the prejudicial effects of indulgence, or fear of discovery and exposure, may adequately protect us from the outward act of sin, so that our conduct in this respect may be blameless. And yet there may be a positive absence of any thing like hatred, or moral dislike, in our feeling against such forms of evil. Perhaps we may even toy with the images of sin, when presented to us by our fancy, or even go so far as to hanker after the removal of restrictions. But God is purity; and, if we do not hate impurity, sicken at the sight and thought of it, and turn away with disgust, it is out of the question that we can love Him.

Again: it is quite possible not to be implicated personally in sin, and yet to treat it, when witnessed or heard of in others, with levity and indifference. While far enough removed from it ourselves, we may speak of it with a smile, and use it to point a jest. This we surely could not do, unless we were indifferent to it; and indifference to it implies that we do not hate it; indifference is a standing aloof from either extreme—equally poised between love and hatred.

If we would realize the full force of the term "hatred of evil," as it ought to exist in all, as it would exist in a perfectly righteous man, we shall do well to consider how sensitive we are to natural evil in its every form—to pain, and suffering, and misfortune. How delicately is the physical frame of man constructed, and how keenly is the slightest derangement in any part of it felt! A little mote in the eye, hardly discernible by the eye of another, the swelling of a small gland, the deposit of a small grain of sand, what agonies may these slight causes inflict! That fine filament of nerves of feeling spread like a wonderful net-work of gossamer over the whole surface of the body, how exquisitely susceptible is it! A trifling burn, or scald, or incision, how does it cause the member affected to be drawn back suddenly, and the patient to cry out! Now, there can be no question that, if man were in a perfect moral state, moral evil would affect his mind as sensibly, and in as lively a manner—would, in short, be as much of an affliction to him, as pain is to his physical frame. He would shrink and snatch himself away, as sin came near to his consciousness; the first entrance of it into his imagination would wound and arouse his moral sensibilities, and make him positively unhappy. You will say, perhaps, that there never was an instance of such acute moral sensibilities in any partaker of our nature. Excuse me; there was. The Holy, Harmless, Undefiled One, Our Lord Jesus Christ, was an instance, and the only instance in point. It was not only that He loathed the grosser forms of evil; but that He flung from Him with abhorrence every unspiritual suggestion, such as that once made to Him by the Apostle Peter, to decline the Cross and consult His own ease. Christ heard the tempter's whisper on that occasion finding an organ for itself in the mouth of the Apostle; but immediately, with that moral indignation which formed one of the grandest elements in His perfect character, the Seed of the Woman turned upon the Serpent, and crushed his head: "Get thee behind Me, Satan: thou art an offence unto me: for thou savorest not the things that be of God, but those that be of men."

And it is this moral sensitiveness of Christ, owing to the perfection of His human nature, which made His sufferings so exquisite and altogether unparalleled, and which probably formed the stress of the trial in His mysterious Agony. As far as the Lord's physical frame went, His sufferings have probably been more than paralleled by those of many of His martyrs. But over and above the torture of crucifixion, there was in the nature of the Lord Jesus a mysterious ground of suffering, which none of us mere sinful men share in common with Him. In the first place, He had lived before His Incarnation from all eternity in a world where sin and sorrow are unknown. Before the morning stars sang together, and all the sons of God shouted for joy, on the occasion of the earth's foundation-stone being laid, the Only Begotten had lain in the bosom of the Father, receiving the incense of the Seraphim's praise. To us sin and sorrow are our familiar native element; they are the notes which have sounded in our ear from infancy, and from their constant repetition have ceased to attract notice; to Him they were a perpetual discord, jarring most offensively with the harmonies of angelic harps. But then again, altogether independently of his Divine extraction, there was in His human nature an avenue by which suffering could reach Him, which in us, alas! sin has closed. This avenue was the moral sensibility of which we have been speaking, a sensibility which, it is true, Grace gradually revives in every character of which it gains the mastery, but which, at the same time, is obtuse in the holiest among us, when compared with the exquisite perfection in which He possessed it. Yet we may reach something of the idea of it, by imagining the case of a very holy man forced into very low and vicious company, and obliged to keep his eyes and his ears open. Imagine an eminent saint who had hitherto lived in habits of close communion with God, thrust not merely into prison, but into such vile society as is usually found in prisons, forced to listen to ribald jests, obscene songs, blasphemous execrations, profane oaths. To the drunkard and the debauchee such society would be no trial; to the saint, even were there no physical discomfort in the circumstances, the mere contact with such company would be a frightful trial. What must it have been, then, to the King of Saints to move amidst wicked and worldly men for thirty-three years; to go up and down in a lazar-house of moral and physical evil, amidst broken hearts, depraved wills, hollow and insincere professions? Fallen man may find such a pilgrimage tolerable; but on His pure spirit surrounding sin exercised at all times a heavy pressure. We can be no judges of His suffering, because we have not naturally the sensibility which alone can enable us to appreciate it; just as one of those animals of simple construction, very low down in the scale of animal life, and with sensations only half developed, could form no notion of the sufferings of a man, whose complex frame is sensitive, and whose mind is exposed to the burden of many anxieties.

In Christ, then, is not only every other grace in perfection, but the perfection of the hatred of evil. And, in conforming the soul to the Image of Christ, the Holy Spirit will form in us, as on the one hand, the love of God, so on the other—that which is indeed only the opposite pole of the love of God—the hatred of evil.

It will be interesting to glance at some exemplifications of this hatred of evil, first in Our Lord, Who is Love, and then in His Apostles.

There can be no question, then, that the first idea which the character of Christ presents to us is that of overflowing love and tender compassion. The Gospel portraiture of Him is that of a gentle lamb, dumb before its shearers. But, if we look a second time into the sacred narratives, we shall find the hatred of sin coming out with no less emphasis than love for the sinner. Never once did a hard word escape Our Lord's lips against those who sinned from infirmity or strength of passion; His hatred of sin in their case was to be manifested by His going among them, taking them by the hand, and drawing them out of the mire. But there were hearts in Judea and Jerusalem, where sin had resolutely intrenched itself within the fortress of hypocrisy; people who were not merely ill-livers, but whose whole life was a lie—people who depraved God's truth, while they professed to teach it, and who did their best to dissuade men from accepting the antidote against evil which the Saviour brought. Understand this well. From simple sin Christ came to save us; and as the way to save us was to win us, and men are not won by being threatened and frightened, you do not hear from His mouth fulminations against the various classes of sinners with which the world abounds, the intemperate, the unclean, the debauched, the dishonest. Sorely did their sins burden His spirit; they even wrung great drops of Blood from His Sacred Person; but He did not say a word, which might be interpreted into a discouragement of those, whom He came to win and save. But against the sin of sins, which impeded and counteracted His saving work, against the false doctrine and hypocrisy of Pharisees, He *did* launch the thunders of His wrath. He did not spare words of censure; He told them in plain terms that the doers of such sins were a brood of hell. "Ye serpents," cried He, "ye generation of vipers, how can ye escape the damnation of hell?" Before His final exit from the Temple He denounced "Woe," nine times, on nine different counts, against characters such as these. Think not that this is derogatory to the Love, which forms the staple of His character. On the contrary, rightly understood, it is a part of His Love. Those who wilfully put obstacles in the way of the salvation of souls are surely the friends of that sin, from which the Lord came to save us. He and His, as they love souls, can have no truce with such persons continuing such endeavors.

I say that neither He *nor His* can have any truce with them. For here His Apostles speak the same language as their Divine Master. When Elymas the sorcerer withstood the Gospel, and sought to turn away Sergius Paulus from the faith, "Saul (who is also called Paul), filled with the Holy Ghost, set his eyes on him, and said, O full of all subtilty and all mischief, thou child of the devil, thou enemy of all righteousness, wilt thou not cease to pervert the right ways of the Lord?" In precisely the same spirit, and for precisely the same reasons, we find St. John, the Apostle of Love, as if to show us that this grace is entirely consistent with a hatred of evil, launching against the heretics of the day, who depraved God's truth by the denial of the Incarnation, this very pointed sentence of excommunication: "He that abideth in the doctrine of Christ, he hath both the Father and the Son. If there come any unto you, and bring not this doctrine, receive him not into your house, neither bid him God speed. For he that biddeth him God speed is partaker of his evil deeds." God's truth is his great instrument for saving souls, and a person who seriously mutilates it in a vital part, deprives it *pro tanto* of efficacy, and thereby does his best to maintain the empire of sin. The Apostle of Love will have no truce with such a one; will not even harbor him under his roof.—Add to this the grand burst of indignation which prematurely terminated the apology of St. Stephen. Resistance to convictions wrought in the heart by the Holy Spirit is not merely sin; but sin stubbornly maintaining its empire in the face of God's attempt to break its power. It is sin intrenching itself in the fortress of the will, and saying to Grace, "Thou shalt not reduce me." St. Stephen, full of holy love, is fired by the thought how often his countrymen had thus resisted God: "Ye stiffnecked," exclaims he, "and uncircumcised in heart and ears, ye do always resist the Holy Ghost: as your fathers did, so do ye." To be a sinner is one thing. Resolutely to maintain sin's empire in ourselves or others is quite a distinct, and a much more deadly, form of evil. Christ and His primitive disciples had only dew and balm for the one. But they had thunder-bolts for the other.

We may here make the general reflection, that Love, as a Christian grace, is an altogether different thing from many qualities which usurp its name. A different thing, first, from that easy pliability of will, which is called good-nature, but which in fact resolves itself into indolence and languor of character. On the contrary, in all real love there is strength, strength of will and strength of character. In all real love there is wrapped up hatred against that evil which counteracts goodness. Without intending for a moment to limit the operations of God's grace, it may be asserted that, generally speaking, the truest Christians have in them the greatest force of character. "The kingdom of heaven," says our Lord, "suffereth violence, and the violent take it by force." There must be resoluteness, in order to obtain such a prize. —And again, He commands that the salt of decision and energy shall be mixed with the oil of love· "Have salt in yourselves;" and as this salt, if it were allowed too great preponderance, might operate to make breaches of the peace, He adds, "Have salt in yourselves, *and have peace one with another*."—And again, Christian love is a very different thing from that indifference to theological error which, in these latitudinarian days, too often apes its manners and mimics its phraseology. In lesser (or doubtful) points, not affecting the vitality of God's truth, our maxim must be tolerance to the very utmost, nay (more than tolerance), a catholic acknowledgment of whatever is good and wise in other Christian Churches. But where the error mutilates the vital parts of the truth, there love can only appear in its form of hatred of evil. It is a very serious breach of love to pay compliments to false doctrine. Our Blessed Lord and His Apostles never did so.

Now let us review summarily our conclusions, and see what light they throw on that question, so vitally affecting our own happiness, Whether or not we love God?

We derive our knowledge of evil from two sources. We find the instigations of it in our own hearts. We see the workings of it in the world around us.

First, then, how are we affected toward the evil which is in ourselves? Do we not merely decline to carry out its instigations in act; but do we reject them with loathing and abhorrence, on the first moment of their being presented to us? Is something more than mere principle enlisted in our resistance to it? is feeling enlisted also?

Next, how are we affected toward it when it appears in others? Do we ever talk of it with a smile or a cynical sneer? Do we, by the sentiments we express, ever encourage the young to imagine that the excesses and vices of youth are at least venial, and entail no real mischief, if not carried beyond youth? Is the society of worldly persons—who estimate all things by a worldly standard, and seem never to breathe a higher element than that which is of the earth, earthy—more and more distasteful to us? How should we favor a counsel, like that given by St. Peter to his Master, to take our ease in this world, and, while steering clear of vice, to abandon the toil and self-sacrifice incidental to God's service and the work of our salvation? Last (but not least), how far have we escaped the latitudinarian tendencies of the time? is our protest against error in principle equally stern with that against vice in practice? or are we, in the true spirit of the age, for a Church where positive dogmas shall be superseded by amiable sentiments to all mankind—a Church which, instead of professing and upholding the mystery of godliness, which is the Catholic Faith once delivered to the Saints, shall glory in professing and upholding nothing beyond those three specious watchwords, which have served as a pretext for the most hideous crimes, Liberty, Fraternity, Equality?

Reader, the love of God involves sympathy with His antipathies. The love of God, as treated of by many devout and pious authors, in whose lucubrations there is much which is edifying and deeply attractive, has worn too much the aspect of a sentiment, or rather of a sentimentalism. A sentiment it is, but a strong and masculine sentiment, as repellent of evil as it is responsive to God's goodness. And it should be a consolation to those who feel themselves at present to be poor proficients in the love of God, if they can at least recognize in themselves a stern resistance to evil. Is not this the way, under the discipline of the Holy Spirit, to master this grace of the love of God? Begin with the negative side, and work up to the positive. Cultivate a hatred of evil, as being offensive to God, and forbidden by Him, and you are cultivating Divine love. As for the sweetness of this love, that is reserved as an encouragement for diligence in getting over the more rugged ground. To feel the love of God exercising a sensible attraction within you, shall be the crown of your efforts, the fragrant blossom which shall grow out of the hatred of evil. Look not for the crown without the cross, nor for the blossom without the thorn.

CHAPTER XIII.

OF PURITY OF MOTIVE.

"*The light of the body is the eye: if therefore thine eye be single, thy whole body shall be full of light. But if thine eye be evil, thy whole body shall be full of darkness. If therefore the light that is in thee be darkness, how great is that darkness!*"—MATT. vi. 22, 23.

THIS figurative saying of Our Lord's occurs in the midst of a paragraph in which He is warning His hearers against the sin of covetousness; and is immediately followed by those well-known words, "No man can serve two masters; for either he will hate the one, and love the other; or else he will hold to the one, and despise the other. Ye cannot serve God *and* mammon." This connection settles conclusively the meaning of the passage. By "the eye" Our Lord must mean the ruling aim or intention. And by "the body" He must mean the whole moral conduct. As the body is habitually governed by the eye—as, when we walk abroad, we move our limbs in obedience to the directions of the eye—so the ruling aim determines our conduct; and often, when we seem to ourselves to do things mechanically and without thought, they are really done in obedience to the ruling aim; just as, when a man walks, he does not think at each step how he shall plant his feet, but simply uses his eyes, and thus walks in safety as a matter of course. The "*single* eye" is doubtless to be interpreted by a reference to what follows, "No man can serve *two* masters." A single eye is one which sees all objects single; as a double eye would be one, the images presented by which are, in consequence of its derangement, double. If a man had such a deranged eye, the members of his body would constantly be misled by its illusions; when he reached forth his hand to an object, he might grasp a phantom; and in walking he might make many a false step, if his sight were confused by two or three images of the road intersecting one another. Now, a person with this bodily complaint is a good image or parable of a man with a double aim or by-end—one who wishes to serve God a little, and the world a little too. He is distracted and misled by a twofold image dancing before his mental eye. And often, when he congratulates himself with some self-complacency on having done a righteous and good action, a thorough scrutiny of his heart and motive would show that he had been only serving his own interests instead of serving his Heavenly Master—seeking human applause, perhaps, not the praise that cometh of God only. By an *evil* eye in the verse following is meant, I believe, not a double intention, but something worse than that, *an intention thoroughly vicious and depraved.* Our Lord describes two extreme spiritual states, the highest and the lowest. The first is characterized by a single eye, i. e., a pure intention in all things to please God out of love. If the eye be thus "single," the intention thus pure, "thy whole body shall be full of light," i. e., every action of yours shall be spiritualized, sanctified, interpenetrated by the luminousness of the intention. The lowest and worst spiritual state is that not of a *double*, which would be intermediate, but of an *evil* eye. This is where the soul intends from perverse motives to do wrong, and was exemplified in the Pharisees, who, though convinced of the truth of Christ's mission, bent their whole strength to put down the truth. Of this latter state He says: "Where the ruling aim is depraved, how dark must the whole lower life of action be, which at best has never any light in itself, but is lit by the ruling aim!" "If the light that is in thee be darkness, how great is the" (not "that") "darkness!"

The words of Our Lord, thus explained, furnish much material for interesting and edifying thought.

First: as to the relation which the intention or ruling aim bears to an action prompted by it. This is defined to be the same relation which the eye bears to the other members of the body. The other members are dark; not only are they not luminous; not only are they not transparent; but there is in them no receptivity for the light; all that they do is to throw back any light which may be shed upon them, or (in other words) to reflect it. And consequently the other members without the eye would be only a gross, dark mass of animal matter, cumbrous, and with no power of self-guidance. But the eye is so constructed as to be receptive of light, and of the images which the light bears on its wings. The images of objects in our neighborhood being presented to us by the eye, we can move our limbs among those objects in safety. Now, the intention with which actions are done is the light, the soul, the eye, the characteristic feature of actions. Yes; the characteristic feature, that is the word; for it is the eye which gives character and expression to the countenance; and it is the intention or aim (and this alone) which gives character or expression to the action. Without any intention, the actions of man become mere dark and confused movements, lit up by no meaning, kindling with no expression.

Indeed, here we come across that broad line of demarcation which separates man from the inferior animals. The inferior animals are agents with a certain freedom of action; but they are not moral agents. Why? Because there is no intention in their actions; nothing higher than the drawing of simple propensions and simple instincts. They are hungry, and they go in quest of their prey; they are thirsty, and they seek water to drink; the maternal instinct makes them shelter their young, and repulse to the best of their power an assailant. But intention, as far as appears (or, in other words, reasonable aim), they have none. It cannot be supposed, for example, that an animal ever takes food with the view of supporting life; he takes food to appease the gnawing of hunger; and there is no reason to imagine that he sees any connection between the taking food and the maintenance of life. I am making a general statement of the case, without asserting that nothing which looks like an exception is anywhere to be found. I do not mean to deny that in some animals instinct struggles up occasionally into a semblance of reason, even as on the borders of the animal and vegetable kingdoms you will find the zoophyte struggling up into the condition of an animal; but anyhow, these efforts of instinct, put them as high as you please, are only temporary, and must be regarded as exceptional. In mere action, then, apart from the rational aim or motive which inspires it, there is no character, no soul, no expression. Take the heroic actions of some pagan as an illustration of what we are saying. Separate the action from the motive; and what becomes of the heroism? Take away the love of country, the love of home and hearth, and the desire of shielding them, take away the love of glory and the thirst for its acquisition—and the gallant exploits of Leonidas and Mettus Curtius are no more exploits—they are merely actions, and actions which brought their perpetrators to a sad and untimely end.

The next point which our passage suggests is, that duplicity of intention—I might say multiplicity of intention—is possible to man from the constitution of his nature.

It seems to be a law running through the whole of Nature that the highest creatures are also most complex in their structure. Vegetables are higher in the scale than mere unorganized matter, and vegetables are of course constructed on a system—are a collection of delicate tubes and fibres, connected with the earth on one hand, and the air on the other. Animals stand on a level above vegetables, and are far more complex in structure, being in fact, in many of their properties, vegetables, only with sensibility and the power of motion superadded. And among animals, the lowest are those whose structure is most simple, where one organ perhaps serves the creature for heart, stomach, liver, and lungs. Then on a loftier platform altogether comes Reason; and reasonable beings are the most complicated of all; for they are in their lower nature both animals and vegetables, only with intelligence, and conscience, and what is called in Scripture "the spirit," superadded.

Now, it is a necessary result of this complexity, if I may so call it, of human nature, that man is liable to the operation of more than one motive in any action. To take the very simplest instance of this, by way of making the idea easier. A man may take food just as an animal does, to appease hunger. But it is clear that he *may* also take it with the view of preserving life and health. Instances frequently occur where food is taken with this intention *only*, and where there is no stimulus of hunger; as when an invalid, whose appetite has failed, is ordered by a physician to take nourishment nevertheless. But in addition to the aim of reason in taking food, there might be (seen beyond, and as it were through, the aim of reason) an aim of religion. The Apostle writes: "Whether therefore ye eat, or drink, or whatsoever ye do, do all to the glory of God." And again: "Every creature of God is good, and nothing to be refused, if it be received with thanksgiving: for it is sanctified by the word of God and prayer." A man *may* take food with the view of tasting, and thereby bringing home to his heart a more lively sense of, the bounty of our Heavenly Father, who daily spreads a table for all His creatures, and by each meal that He provides answers the Christian's Prayer, "Give us this day our daily bread." He may also take it with the view of making his body a fitter and more efficient instrument of the Divine service, a view which would effectually preclude all intemperate use of God's gifts, and make a man's real need the law of his appetite. This is the simplest instance I can find of several motives, which might prompt one and the same action. But this complexity of motives is seen in almost every action that we do. Those who knew most of human life and of their own hearts, know that *very, very rarely indeed* is any action done from one single motive. If pleasure or recreation be the main object, there is generally a thought also (except in the very young or very frivolous) of some usefulness in the action, as (for example) that it is of use to recruit the mind for serious pursuits. And, conversely, whenever an action is done as a duty, and mainly out of a sense of duty, there are scarcely ever wanting additional stimulants to it, in the shape of the approbation of conscience or the approbation of other men.

And these last words suggest a thought, which it will be much to the purpose of our argument slightly to expand. There is one fertile source of complexity of motive in human actions, which must receive a distinct notice. This source is the relations of man to society—relations these again, by which he is distinguished from the inferior animals. In every thing that we say or do (that is, in all our outward conduct), we are under some regard to what our little world will say or think of our actions. Man is made for society; and one evidence of this is, that there is in the constitution of his mind such a constant reference to the views and sentiments of his neighbors. But then this constant reference, though it is an admirable social safeguard, is very apt to confuse and disturb religious purity of intention. My susceptibility to human praise and blame, of which I find it so extremely difficult to rid myself, may be the greatest of all snares to me in the spiritual life. Grant that I do a certain action with the view of pleasing God. But is this view really and truly the only view which is influencing me? Have I no other spring of energy but the sole desire of pleasing Christ? Is my eye single? Should I do the action, or should I do it with the same zest and interest, if no eyes were upon me but God's only? Certain it is that the eyes of my neighbors do exert a most real influence, do fascinate me with a real spell, of which it is exceedingly hard to disenchant myself. And this circumstance should make me suspicious of myself at best, however much I may think that I have cleansed my heart of all but the highest motive. Take the case of attendance upon the ordinances of God. The society in which we move exercises in this particular so marked a restraint upon the conduct of poor and rich, that, from the mere fact of a man's coming to church, one can conclude nothing as to his coming from a spiritual motive. In the country you will find many regular church-goers among the poor, who, when they migrate to London, and locate themselves in some alley or mews, never cross the sacred threshold from year's end to year's end. What is the account of this inconsistency of conduct? It is very simple. Eyes were upon them in the country parish, the eye of the magistrate, the eye of the squire, the eye of the vicar, which are now removed. They had no single intention of approving themselves in their church-going to the all-seeing Eye; otherwise, as that Eye sees them in their garret in the mews, no less than it saw them in their rustic cottage, they would come to church still. Nor is the attendance of the rich upon religious ordinances one whit less apt to be flawed by duplicity of motive than that of the poor. In England a man will be regular and punctual in his attendance. But what is his regularity and punctuality worth? You shall see, when he gets to a foreign country, where he is quite out of the reach of his visiting acquaintance, and where observance of the Sunday is generally disregarded. He takes his tone abroad from the foreigners, as he took his tone at home from his own countrymen. He gets lax in his religious habits, soon rubs off his scruples about pleasuring on Sunday, thinks it enough to drop into a church occasionally and tolerate the sermon; and, if his stay in those parts is prolonged for two or three years, he comes back to his native land a church-goer no longer. His service done to the Almighty in His House formerly was such as the Apostle proscribes in those pregnant words: "Not with eye-service, as men-pleasers."

We have now seen that perfect purity of intention is the highest spiritual state, a state which probably the holiest man has never reached, but to which all real children of God are in different measures approximating. Are we striving for this purity of intention, praying for it, laboring for it, seeking to bring the whole of our spiritual life up to this standard? It is something—nay, it is much—to have a right discernment of the standard in the spiritual life. Now, the standard is this, that all things should be done from the love of Christ, and a consequent desire to please Him, and that we should act singly from this motive. Real Christians do a large number of things which are right. But there is still great room for improvement in these right things; for there is much defectiveness of intention in them; and this defectiveness of intention may be, by self-examination, and careful attention, and prayer, remedied.

1st. By self-examination. Let the motives, as well as the actions, be scrutinized in self-examination. Many and many an action of the Christian looks, like an apple of Sodom, fair and attractive externally, the heart of which is rotten, and which crumbles into dust when we press upon its interior. Let us habitually apply, to actions which are outwardly righteous, the crucial questions: "Should I have done this, or done it with equal zeal, had no eye of man been upon me? Should I have resisted this temptation if there had been no check upon me from human law or public opinion? Should I have acted thus faithfully and conscientiously without the stimulus of human praise?"

2dly. By self-discipline and care. Let us cultivate particularly, and strive to acquit ourselves well in, those actions of the Christian Life which are in their nature private, and cannot come abroad. For example, private prayer and private study of the Scriptures. Exercises such as these are more or less a satisfactory test of religious character, because they are incapable of being prompted by human respect. No eye of man is upon us when we enter into our closet, and shut our door, and pray to our Father which is in secret; and therefore here it would seem no motive but a religious one can well intrude. And we may apply the same remark to all the ordinary actions and commonplace business of life, which must be transacted by all in some way, and may be transacted by the Christian with a spiritual intention. What does growing in grace mean, but that this spiritual intention should lengthen its reach—should extend itself more and more to every corner of our life? Some little business of routine calls my attention at a certain hour, having nothing sublime or extraordinary in it, but the neglect of which would entail discomfort and annoyance—a visit, or a letter of courtesy, or an interview, in which a few necessary words pass, and then it is over. Well; even the most earthly of earthly actions, those which are most bound up with this transitory state of things, and which have no intrinsic dignity or sacredness whatever, may be spiritualized by importing into them a spiritual intention. The little courtesies, for example, which society requires, may be yielded simply because they *are* social requirements, in which case they will be often done "grudgingly, and of necessity;" or they may be regarded as so many opportunities of compliance with the inspired precept, "Be courteous" —in which case they will be done cheerfully, "as to the Lord, and not unto men." And (generally) the meeting all calls upon us, however humble, with the thought that they come to us in the way of God's Providence, and in the working out of the system of things which He has appointed, and are indications of the quarter in which He would have us direct our energies, is a great means of purifying our intention, and so of advancing in spirituality. For nobody is aware what is going on in our hearts, when we meet these calls in a devout spirit; our friends only see us doing commonplace things which others do, and give us no credit. But, in so meeting such calls, we have praise of God, who, like a good Father, marks with a smile of approbation the humblest efforts of His children to please Him.

I have traced the bearing of the subject on our Sanctification. But I must not omit to call attention to its bearing on our Justification also. It is possible that a man, who judges himself by his outward conduct exclusively, might think with some complacency of his devout, regular, reputable life. But no man can do so who, laying to heart Our Lord's maxim that the intention determines the character of actions, brings his heart with all its motives to the touchstone of God's Word. Then it is, if the Holy Spirit cooperates with his self-examination, that, catching sight of the miserable shortcomings even of his virtues and his devotions, he exclaims with the Prophet: "All our righteousnesses are as filthy rags." And then it is that he looks about for a ground of acceptance with God wholly independent of his own righteousness, and, finding this assured and stable ground in the obedience to the Second Adam unto death, plants himself upon that ground exclusively, never more to shift therefrom; and, in his transactions with a holy and heart-searching God, puts forward no plea of merit but that which is contained in those precious, pregnant words of another Prophet: "*The Lord our Righteousness.*"

The connection of singleness of aim with the subject of the present work, which is the pursuit and attainment of Holiness, will I think be apparent. To live holily is nothing else than, in every thing we do, to act from a single desire to please God, out of love to Him, and from no other aim whatever. The more we can succeed in stripping ourselves bare of every motive save this highest one, the nearer shall we be to the standard at the attainment of which we are aiming. A double-minded man is unstable in all his ways; a heart divided between two motives, halting between two opinions, cannot plant its steps firmly in the way of righteousness. Nor let any one who seeks after this simplicity of motive, and sincerely endeavors to do all (even the most trivial) things, "not with eye-service as a men-pleaser, but as a servant of Christ, doing the will of God from the heart," be dismayed by finding that only a very partial success attends his early efforts. By constant watchfulness, much ejaculatory prayer, and at first a somewhat stern recalling of the mind from its wanderings to its centre, progress will be made slowly though surely. God never fails to prompt and teach a soul, which is simply desirous of pleasing Him. He will, if we are faithful to Him, show us how to escape the snares of a morbid self-consciousness and scrupulosity, which seem to the eye of the natural man to beset the path we are advocating, and which it is too true the Devil knows how to set. A man with his eyes in a right condition does not, when he walks, study every step he takes, nor even make the reflection that he is using his eyes; but he guides himself instinctively by his eyes, and with their help enjoys the landscape. And a man, whose ruling aim is right and single, comes at last, through all perplexity, to feel that God's service, so far from being a bondage of oppressive restraints, is perfect freedom, and that the only true way (as the Psalmist indicates) "of walking at liberty" is, "to seek His commandments."

CHAPTER XIV.

PEACE OF CONSCIENCE AND OF HEART THE ELEMENT OF HOLINESS.

"*Now the Lord of peace Himself give you peace always by all means.*"—2 THESS. iii. 16.

"ALWAYS." The Apostle is imploring for his Thessalonian converts a state of mind which shall be absolutely permanent, which shall know of no intermission. The same expression is used where Our Lord says of the little ones, that their guardian angels do ALWAYS behold the face of God; and again where St. Peter represents Christ as saying in the words of David, "I foresaw the Lord ALWAYS before my face." The constancy of the Christian's peace, then, is to be the same constancy wherewith angels wait on the behests of God, wherewith the Lord Jesus Himself perpetually realized God's Presence.

And again: "Give you peace *by all means*"—literally, "*in every manner.*" Thus he says of the preaching of Christ among the Philippians, which in some instances did not proceed from a pure motive: "Notwithstanding EVERY WAY, whether in pretence or in truth, Christ is preached." There are different modes in which, different circumstances under which, the peace that reigns in the Christian's heart will be manifested; peace will take a somewhat different form, according as the heart is burdened with anxiety, or depressed by a sense of sin, or feverish with excitement, or distracted by business; and the Apostle prays that the Thessalonians may taste it *in every form*, according to the special need of the moment.

Once more: "The Lord of Peace" (He who is its Author, and the Source from which it flows) is here called upon to bestow it: "The Lord of peace Himself GIVE you peace." Quite consistently with those words of Our Lord, wherein He communicates peace as His legacy to His disciples: "Peace I leave with you, my peace *I give* unto you: not as the world giveth, give I unto you." And then He immediately goes on to recognize a certain power in the heart (with His aid, and by His grace) to quiet *itself*, a certain self-control which it must exercise in order to realize the blessing; for He adds: "Let not your heart be troubled, neither let it be afraid." And the same power of self-control in the Christian himself is recognized in the beautifully soothing words of St. Paul to the Philippians: "*Be careful for nothing*" (it lies with us, therefore, to harbor anxieties, or to dismiss them); "but in every thing by prayer and supplication with thanksgiving let your requests be made known unto God" (that is, do *your* part simply and faithfully by recommending your wants to God); "and" (then God shall do His, the Author of peace and Lover of concord shall confer upon you the blessing, which by your own exertions you could never have attained) "the peace of God, which passeth all understanding, shall keep your hearts and minds through Christ Jesus."—"*Hearts and minds;*" here is another valuable idea necessary to our conceiving the subject in its fulness. Peace is needed for *heart* and *mind* both, for the conscience which is apt to be burdened; for the affections and feelings which are apt to be harassed, wounded, thwarted; and for the thoughts, which are apt to stray out of the precinct of sobriety, to rove to forbidden subjects, to indulge in vain anticipations, to pursue curious and unprofitable speculations.

The peace of which we have been speaking is a main essential to Holiness. It is not only the root out of which Holiness grows, but the strength in which alone it can be successfully pursued, and the element in which it moves. Its grand importance is very emphatically recognized by our Book of Common Prayer. As a standing part of the daily Morning and Evening Office we have a Collect for Peace, which in the Order of Morning Prayer stands before the Collect for Grace. The *Evening* Collect for Peace came originally toward the close of the Service, and, together with "Lighten our darkness," formed the Church's requiem for her children, before they laid them down to rest. But see how clearly this noble collect recognizes the truth that Peace is essential to Holiness: "Give unto Thy servants that peace which the world cannot give; *that our hearts may be set to obey Thy commandments.*" The firm resolution, in God's strength, to serve Him, and to abide by His will, whatever may come of it, cannot be maintained, while heart, conscience, mind, are in a turbid state. In a violent storm, the needle of the compass is so agitated that no direction can be had from it, the vessel's head cannot be set right. And, when the inner man is agitated by storms of passion, or apprehension, or by a sense of sin, it is difficult, if not impossible, to rectify the intention, and to make the mind's needle point true. Christ must say to the internal tumult, as of old to the winds and waves, "Peace, be still;" and, when He has made a great calm, we may then rectify our aim, and set forth on our voyage with renewed effort.

We will speak very briefly in this Chapter of two forms of peace which are essential to the pursuit of Holiness, leaving the discussion of other forms for consideration in future Chapters.

I. First: in order to Holiness, it is absolutely necessary that peace should both be admitted into the *conscience*, and maintained there.

To *admit* it, there must be a genuine act of faith in the blood and righteousness of Christ—such an act as shall shed abroad in the heart a sense of God's pardoning love, and dissipate effectually the dread of His displeasure. This act of faith is simply a cordial acceptance of God's gift of Christ—an opening of the windows of the soul to the glorious, animating sunlight of Divine Love. Having performed this act, we place ourselves in the condition described by St. Paul, when he says, "Therefore being justified by faith, we have *peace* with God through our Lord Jesus Christ."

But the admission of peace once for all is by no means sufficient; it must be *detained*, after being once received. Peace is a very sensitive guest, apt to take flight at the slightest affront. The conscience, once cleared by faith, must be kept clear by effort, and the use of appropriate means, and (crowning all these) by repeated acts of the faith which once cleared it. We must brace our spiritual system by healthy exercise—the exercise which St. Paul, the apostle of faith, professes that he never intermitted: "And herein do I exercise myself, to have always a conscience void of offence toward God and toward men."

But as faults will accrue, notwithstanding all our efforts, and as, the more we advance in the spiritual life, the more sharp-eyed we shall become to our faults, and the more they will distress us, we shall need, in order to the maintenance of peace, periodical examinations of the conscience, and a periodical opening of the heart to God on the subject of what we find there. Under certain circumstances it may be advantageous to reveal the secrets of the conscience to some spiritual counsellor, partly to humble ourselves the more thereby, partly to gain advice suitable to our needs, and partly to secure an interest in his prayers. In cases where a man is conscious of grievous secret sins, while he has enjoyed a reputation for piety, he will often be led to feel that such a confession to man is essential to his peace—that peace can in no wise consist with the consciousness of hypocrisy; that in no other way can he be at one with God than by being at one with truth. And, as regards cases which have not this feature, let it be remembered that one reason why the sermons of the clergy are so pointless is, that they are so rarely admitted into the confidence of their people; and that, if there were more unreserve in laying bare to them the difficulties which we experience in our spiritual course, the more would the help which there may be in them, whether from their study of God's Word, or from the commission with which they are armed, be turned to account—however, this discipline of private confession, though under particular circumstances *recommended* by our own Church, is certainly not made *obligatory*, either by the Scriptures or the Book of Common Prayer. But, fully admitting this, it must still be said that we can never safely discard a periodical examination of conscience, with an exposure of its secrets to, and a discharge of its burdens upon, our great High Priest. This is a part of spiritual discipline, to which they who will not be at the pains to submit are only too likely to drop into a habit of general unwatchfulness, and laxity, and neglect of devotion—a habit most congenial to our natural love of ease, and entirely falling in with the smooth, self-indulgent temper of our age.

II. The second form of peace, which must be maintained in order to Holiness, is peace in the *heart* —peace under the vexations and fretting of life.

(1) This fretting may arise first from anxieties. The right method of dealing with anxieties, and maintaining peace of heart under them, is clearly and succinctly laid down by St. Paul in the passage already quoted from the Philippians. Whatever may be your wishes on the subject which makes you anxious, refer them to God in prayer (using the simplest and most direct language), not asking Him absolutely to bring them about, which might be productive of any thing but a happy result, but simply letting Him know them, and begging Him to deal in the matter, not according to your short-sighted views, but

as seems best to His wisdom and love. This exposure of the heart's wishes to God is a fulfilment of the precept: "Trust in Him at all times, ye people; pour out your hearts before Him;" it is acting in the spirit of Hezekiah, when he went up into the temple and spread Sennacherib's letter before the Lord. Having made this reference of your wishes to God, leave them with Him, in confident assurance that He will order the matter for the best. I say, *leave them* with Him. Drop them altogether. Do not let your mind recur to them any more; they are off your hands now; they are in better hands than yours; they are no longer your business, and therefore they need not—nay, they must not—be your care. If prudence and caution dictate that any thing should be done to avert the evil you anticipate, do it, and then think no more of the subject. Thinking of it is utterly fruitless: "Which of you by taking thought can add one cubit unto his stature?" And fruitless thinking is just so much waste of that mental and spiritual energy, every atom of which you need for your spiritual progress. But it is worse than this. It is a positive breach of God's precept, "Be careful for nothing"—that is, do not give anxiety a harbor in your heart; let it not find there a peg to hang its burden on. Deal with a fruitless anxiety just as you would deal with an impure or a resentful motion of the heart. Shut the door on it at once, and with one or two short ejaculatory prayers rouse the will, and turn the thoughts in a different direction. The spiritual life of the present moment is the one thing needful; as for the evil in the future, that may never come; and, if it does, you will probably find that it has been far worse in anticipation than it is in the reality. The holy women on their road to Christ's sepulchre anticipated a difficulty which threatened to baffle entirely their pious design. "Who shall roll us away the stone," they said among themselves, "from the door of the sepulchre?" It turned out that they were troubled about nothing. When they marched up close to it, the difficulty had vanished. "When they looked," says the Evangelist, "they saw that the stone *was* rolled away." Take encouragement from their example. Go forward in your spiritual course with all the energy of your soul. Place the foreseen difficulties in the hand of God, and He shall remove them.

(2) Secondly: fretting and discomposure of heart may result from things going cross in daily life, from rubs of temper, offences, irritation, and annoyance with others. The rule for the maintenance of peace is here the same. Never let your thoughts dwell on a matter in which another has made you sore. If you do, a hundred aggravating circumstances will spring up in your mind, which will make the slightest offence swell up to the most formidable dimensions. With a brief prayer for him who has offended you, keep your thoughts sedulously away from what he has done. Try to realize God's Presence; the realizing it ever so little has a wonderfully soothing and calming influence on the heart. "My Presence shall go with thee," said God to Moses; and then immediately adds, as if that were a necessary consequence of the foregoing, "and I will give thee *rest*." But the great point is to let the mind settle. Turbid liquids will clear themselves, and precipitate their sediment to the bottom simply by standing. Be still, then. Refrain from

every impulsive action and speech. Make an effort to turn the mind, till it is perfectly cool and reasonable, to other subjects. Say secretly, "The Lord is in His Holy Temple" (His temple of the inner man); "keep silence, O my heart, before Him."

Those who indulge fretful feelings, either of anxiety, or irritation, know not what an opening they thereby give to the devil in their hearts. "Fret not thyself," says the Psalmist; "*else shalt thou be moved to do evil.*" And in entire harmony with this warning of the elder Scriptures is the precept of St. Paul against undue indulgence of anger: "Let not the sun go down upon your wrath, *neither give place to the devil.*" Peace is the sentinel of the soul, which keeps the heart and mind of the Christian through Christ Jesus. So long as this sentinel is on guard and doing his duty, the castle of the soul is kept secure. But let the sentinel be removed, and the way is opened immediately for an attack upon the fortress. And our spiritual foes are vigilant, however much we may sleep. They are quick to observe an opportunity, and prompt to avail themselves of it. They rush upon the city at once in the absence of the sentinel, and do great mischief in a short time.

In conclusion: be careful to maintain peace in the heart, if thou wouldst not only resist the devil, but also receive the guidance of God's Spirit. That Spirit cannot make communications to a soul in a turbulent state, stormy with passion, rocked by anxiety, or fevered with indignation. The Lord is neither in the great and strong wind, nor in the earthquake, nor in the fire; and not until these have subsided and passed away, can His still small voice be heard communing with man in the depths of his soul.

CHAPTER XV.

PEACE BY LIVING IN THE PRESENT RATHER THAN IN THE PAST.

"*And He said unto another, Follow Me. But he said, Lord, suffer me first to go and bury my father. Jesus said unto him, Let the dead bury their dead: but go thou and preach the kingdom of God.*"—LUKE ix. 59, 60.

WE saw in our last Chapter that peace of heart and mind is essential to Holiness; and we traced two of the forms in which this peace manifests itself, reserving for future consideration its other forms. Peace amid the various distractions of heart and mind, incidental to our nature and circumstances, will form the subject of this and the following Chapter.

We shall never know what it is to live in peace, until we know what it is to live thoroughly in the present. The assertion startles some of my readers. But let them look at it again; and they will see no reason for surprise or alarm. A preposition will sometimes make the whole difference in the meaning of a proposition. I do not say that, in order to the maintenance of peace, we should live FOR the present—God forbid! (Dives in one parable, and the rich man whose ground brought forth plentifully in another, did so, and tasted not a spiritual, but a carnal peace, which only deserves the name of *ease*, a name actually given to it in the latter case: "Soul, take thine *ease*, eat, drink, and be merry.") My assertion was that we should live IN the present, and that, until we have learned to do so, we cannot taste of peace. The present has its duties, which are imperative and pressing. We need all the energy of our souls (we have never more energy than we can spare; oh! how do the holy angels in heaven, whose spirits are always so fervent, though the debt they owe to God is trifling in comparison of ours, put to shame the sad lack of energy in the best of us!)—I say, we need all our energy for the fulfilment of present duties. Christ has said to each of us at our Baptism, and in our Confirmation—is saying still by His warnings, His ministers, and the inspiration of His Spirit (although in a sense different from that in which He addressed the words to certain persons in the days of His earthly pilgrimage): "Follow Me." Morning by morning He says to us, as we wake up refreshed, and a new day, full of hope and promise, dawns upon us by His long-suffering mercy: "Follow Me." The task thus imposed is of quite sufficient magnitude and difficulty to absorb all our faculties. It cannot possibly be done as a by-work. It cannot be done in the same way as busy professional men (and sometimes statesmen) occupy their leisure moments with the relaxations of literature. The following of Christ cannot be taken up as a relief or ornamental appendage to our life; it must be our main business, or it is fruitless to take it up at all. And observe that, being spiritual, it makes a large demand upon the mental powers; more mind, more processes of thought and feeling, have to be thrown into the following of Christ than into any other pursuit in the world. This being so, the Christian's heart and mind must not suffer from distractions, if he is to follow Christ successfully. The whole of the heart and mind are needed for the present pursuit, which is always, in one shape or another, under one vocation or another, the following of the Lord Jesus. Such must be the rule therefore for the spiritual man: "Whatsoever thy hand findeth to do, do it with thy might." Live IN the present.

But alas! the habit of the natural man, the tendency of every mind, so far as it is unrenewed by God's Holy Spirit, is to live either in the past or in the future—to look back with fond and longing regret to former days and interests which have faded with time; or else to look forward to some such change of circumstances or position as offers to give a relief and a rest which we do not experience at present. To the first of these distractions the old, to the second the young, are more especially exposed. Both have a tendency to sap that peace which lies at the root of Holiness, and which, neither wasting vain regrets over yesterday, nor aspiring to a brighter to-morrow, is content with the PRESENT, and strives to make it available for Christ's Service to the utmost.

We will consider only the first of these distractions at present—the distraction of a fond and mournful retrospect. In minds of a certain temperament a good deal of thinking and feeling runs to waste in this direction.

Our Lord had observed in one of His disciples (for St. Matthew expressly calls the person in question "a disciple ") a tendency to relax in his attendance upon Him, and perhaps to return to the domestic ties and the worldly pursuit which, at Christ's first summons, he had quitted. Reading the man's thoughts, His Divine Master laid upon him the call a second time more peremptorily: "Follow Me." This elicited the feelings which were working in his mind. He pleaded his father's death, the intelligence of which he had recently received, and the duty of natural piety arising therefrom, as a reason, not for ultimately declining Christ's call, but for postponing *immediate* compliance with it. But he was needed as God's instrument to give life to dead souls, not to consign to the grave dead bodies; and those members of his family who had not been, as he had, quickened into new convictions and spiritual life, might suffice to perform the duties of sepulture: "Let the dead bury their dead; but go thou and preach the Kingdom of God."

We cannot so understand the Lord of Love, who rebuked with severity Jewish evasions of the Fifth Commandment, and who amid the tortures of the Cross made provision for His own Virgin Mother, as to suppose that He intended to discourage the plainest duties of natural affection. He spoke startlingly and almost paradoxically, as His manner was, in order to arouse thought; and His words are to be understood, as they so often are, in their spirit and principle rather than their letter. And their spirit and principle is this: "A sentiment of nature, however just, must not be allowed to interfere with a spiritual call; nor must a fond, lingering regret, for that which in the order of God's Providence has passed away, detain us for a single moment from the duty of the PRESENT." Let us expand the precious thought which Christ thus gives us, in reference to the subject which we are pursuing.

I observe, first, that all things (and not men and women only) have their time; and, their time having expired, die a natural death. "The fashion of this world passeth away." Childhood, with its many graces, its innocence, its simplicity, its prattle, its ingenuous ways, lasts but a short time; beautiful in its season, it is as transient as the first violet of spring; the children grow up, and become young men and women, sophisticated with the ways of the world.—Again: opinions and ways of looking at a subject are in a continual state of flux; old opinions are always fading out, and new opinions (new lights, as some call them, new schools of thought, as others) are constantly forming and unfolding themselves, and, after they have had a certain run, waning again, and losing their hold upon men's minds. The political and religious controversies of the present day are not those of our youth; controversy has shifted its ground since we were children, has left its old questions, as if they were no more of interest, and now rages, with all its old rage, round a new set of topics. Institutions, too, are subject to the common lot of mortality; even those which in their day exercised the widest influence, and which men took the greatest pains to root in the earth, under the impression that they would make them permanent, find themselves, in the progress of thought and civilization, supplanted by new machineries, not as picturesque or poetical it may be; but doing the work which they formerly did, in a way more adapted to the spirit of the times. To take one of a thousand instances which might be referred to: monasteries, which in dark and semi-barbarous mediæval days were, notwithstanding all the abuses incidental to them, the great nurseries of Charity, Learning, and Devotion, have long since done their work, and yielded to the law of natural decay; and have given place (in respect of the benefits which they conferred upon mankind) to agencies of a modern style, Poor-laws, Hospitals, Religious Societies, Printing-presses, Public Libraries, and so forth. It is *only the principles* of Truth, Goodness, and Right, which are to last forever. The forms, in which these exhibit themselves, will necessarily vary with the age, and state of society.

But it is quite the habit of the natural mind—and it is a habit adverse to peace, and to the maintenance of spirituality—to look back upon the past (whether our own individual past, or that of society) with a fond, longing regret. We all have something of Lot's wife in us; we linger in our course to take one more retrospect of what has attached itself to us by old associations, but is now doomed. To begin with the changes undergone by society. There are some (and these men of piety and learning, actuated by the best intentions) who avowedly aim at bringing back the monastic system, and try (I cannot say, to resuscitate, but) to galvanize the conventual life, at all events to exhibit the outward show of it to the amazed eyes of men far on in the nineteenth century. But the monastic system, an excellent instrument for the age in which it was the one great agency of the Church, is now effete altogether. Nor can we with any profit or advantage allow ourselves to regret its many noble features, much less to create what, after all our efforts, will be only a caricature of it. It was natural in its own age; it is unnatural now. "Let the dead bury their dead;" and go thou to do thy work for Christ, in the midst of a crooked and perverse generation, with the new implements—Churches, Schools, Hospitals, or whatever they be—which God hath put into thy hand. Then, as to these new forms of thought, which are fermenting all around us, and to which the older among us find some difficulty in adjusting our opinions. No doubt, looking to the awful disclosures made by Holy Scripture respecting the great Apostasy from the Faith, which shall be a feature of the latter days, and looking also at the revolutionary and lawless tendency of the age, as shown in political and social movements, *we are quite right in regarding with suspicion, and in narrowly questioning and examining, all new-fangled views, whether religious or social.* And yet there should be a readiness in us, though not to abandon for one moment the old truth, yet to recognize any new form in which it may be presented. We have been brought up to regard truth—religious, and it may be political and social truth also—in one aspect. But Truth is many-sided, like a cube; and we should never be so tenacious of the aspect of it, which is familiar to us, as not to be ready to come round and view it under another man's aspect. And as for lamenting that progress of thought, which is continually presenting the truth in different aspects, such lamentations are as foolish as they are fruitless. Must the forms of thought, which satisfied men in a former generation, necessarily content us now? Before they can be expected to do so, you must lay a prohibition upon the intellectual growth of the species, and bid the human mind, as Joshua bade the sun, stand still.

But to come closer home to the individual Christian. The past of our own life has a peculiar fascination for us. We think of the days of our childhood, and the scenes of our home, with a natural tenderness; it seems to us that we were then innocent, pure, thoroughly happy. And farther on in life, too, every old and familiar association has a natural charm for us; never can we experience again (as we think) so great happiness as in that little house, in which we first began domestic life; never can any friendships be so attractive as those with which we were then surrounded; never again can the children be so dear, as when they were altogether children; and as for those whom we have loved and lost, we linger over their memories as if they could never have equals; and thus we muse on in the vein of natural sentiment, wasting thereby the mental energy which is needed for the present following of JESUS:

> "Oh for the touch of a vanished hand,
> And the sound of a voice that is still!
> Break, break, break,
> At the foot of thy crags, O Sea!
> But the tender grace of a day that is dead
> Will never come back to me."

"A day that is dead"—all days, when they have done their work, die of themselves. But shall we hang over the corpse of them in fruitless regret, as if there were no such good days (a heart-breaking thought) in store for our hereafter? What saith the Law? "*Thou shalt not eat that which dieth of itself;*" there is no wholesome mental food in a melancholy retrospect of that which has passed away in the natural order of things. And what say the Prophets? "I have spread out my hands unto a rebellious people . . . a people that provoketh Me to anger continually to My face; *which remain among the graves, and lodge in the monuments.*" The Loving Lord, Who invites us to His Bosom in penitence and faith, will not have us linger mournfully among the graves of the past, or lodge our heart's best affections in the monuments of days departed. And what saith the Gospel? "Let the dead bury their dead; but go thou and preach the Kingdom of God." Dead souls, and only dead souls, can afford time for pathetic plaints over an age that is dead; as for living souls, the call to them is instant and urgent to do the work of God's Kingdom, assured that the full establishment of that Kingdom will gild the future with a brighter ray, a "tenderer grace," than any which decks the past.

But to drop figures and use quite plain speech. Sentiment, if it be sound and pure, is an excellent thing; it elevates and refines the soul. But, in order to be sound and pure, *sentiment must be in accordance with truth.* Now, the sentiment which hangs over the past with an excessive fondness is *not* in accordance with truth. The past seems to us *now* faultless and bright. But we know for certain that it was not so. The past days, whether of society or of the individual, had their sins and sorrows, like all other days, which grievously blurred and marred them. The days of our childhood look innocent and happy in the retrospect; but in real fact we had faults and troubles then as well as now, although on a scale suitable to our age. In old times men were *not* better or wiser upon the whole than they are now; Virtue and Piety have *not* taken their flight from the earth; no, nor even Poetry, nor Chivalry, nor Romance; but these things, according to the law of God's Providence—a law of constant decay and renascence—exhibit themselves in a shape different from what they wore yesterday. Our memory has a trick of deceiving us as to the true state of the case. While the present is always dull and prosaic, memory sheds round the past the softening hues of the imagination. There is an optical illusion something similar to this. A landscape which is very tame and bald when we are plodding through the midst of the country, looks more interesting in the blue distance, its plain and hard features being softened away.

Let not any man think so poorly of the Kingdom of God, as to imagine that it will not over-abundantly repay all who work for it or in it. At the wedding-festival with which His Ministry opened, the Lord created toward the close of the entertainment wine, which exceeded in richness and flavor any that the guests had hitherto tasted. And if, dismissing all vain and enervating regrets, we do but labor now with singleness of purpose for the coming of His Kingdom in our own hearts, and (as far as we have opportunity) in the hearts of others, He, the Heavenly Bridegroom, will give us even now such foretastes of joy, and will in the end pour into our souls such an influx of blessedness, that, at every fresh draught of the rivers of His pleasures, we shall disparage all previous satisfactions in comparison of that which we are at present tasting, and shall say with the governor of the feast at Cana: "Thou hast kept the good wine until now."

CHAPTER XVI.

PEACE BY LIVING IN THE PRESENT RATHER THAN IN THE FUTURE.

"*Be content with such things as ye have.*"—Heb. xiii. 5.

IN the last Chapter we considered one of the great distractions which hinder peace of mind, and therefore hinder Holiness, in the soul of man—the distraction of a fond and mournful retrospect. We saw how such a retrospect deludes us—what tricks the memory plays in making a pleasing and attractive picture of by-gone days, and how she throws over the past the softening tints of the imagination. In truth, the various scenes of our life resemble that to which they have been so often compared, the scenes of a theatre. In order that the effect of such scenes may be pleasing, they must be viewed from a distance. Approach them closely, and you see that they are coarsely painted on a large, rude scale, and that the perspective lines, which should carry the eye into the distance, run up into the air; but fall back a few yards, and place yourself in the seats of the spectators, and the coloring loses all its coarseness, and the picture seems no more flat. So it is with our experiences of life. "'Tis distance lends enchantment to the view."

The distraction which we are now to consider is that which arises from living in the future—from pressing forward in desire to some better, easier, more satisfying state than that in which we at present find ourselves.

This habit of mind is very early developed; and yet it does not lose its hold upon us, until we are past middle age, and the winter of life has settled down upon us. In youth the heart bounds up at the prospect of the future; for life has many pleasures to offer to the young, of which experience has not yet proved the hollowness. What boy has not longed to become a man, to be emancipated from the restraints of education, and to be his own master? What young man, not yet embarked in any regular pursuit, has not longed to enter upon his profession and to settle in life? And what man, plunged in life's business and turmoil, has not sighed for the period when his affairs will allow him to retire, and to enjoy rest at the close of his career?

But if this tendency to press forward to some better and more satisfactory future is always seen in human nature, whatever its circumstances, it is most especially seen in the present age, which, perhaps beyond any other, develops and foments it. The age is a most restless one—restless to a morbid and unnatural degree. The ease and speed with which we are able to travel, the ease and speed with which thought can be communicated from one part of the world to another, the wide spread of education, which is ever making the lower class tread upon the heels of the higher, the competition which arises from the fact of all pursuits and professions being overstocked, and which makes the whole of life a race, in which victory is to the swift and strong, and the slow and weak are pushed aside and trampled under foot—all these circumstances create an atmosphere of high pressure and excitement, which, if we mix with men at all, it is impossible not to breathe. And the result of breathing it is, that we come to consider every stage in life only as a step to a further stage; that each man says to himself (not avowedly, of course, but in the general tendency and bias of his mind): "I must rise in life. I must first and before all things else get on. I must push, and thrust, and jostle until my neighbor falls back, and I stand in advance of him. I do not recognize that I have any fixed place assigned to me by God's Providence, and to which more especially my natural capacities are adapted; but there is a variety of places, in all of which God may be served; and the motto for me is, 'The higher the better.' As for settling down in any one position, and saying, 'Here I limit all my desires and aspirations,' that cannot be until just the close of life."

But let us look at this tendency of mind for a moment in the light which is lent by Holy Scripture. "Having food and raiment," says the Apostle Paul, "let us be therewith content." And again more searchingly, because the reference is not to the supply of mere material wants, but to a general change of condition: "Let every man abide in the same calling wherein he was called. . . . . Brethren, let every man, wherein he is called, therein abide with God." And again in the passage which stands at the head of this Chapter: "Be content with such things as ye have;" an inexact translation, however, not conveying a sense by any means so stringent as the original, which is, "Be content with *the things that are present*" (that is, not only with the amount of property which has fallen to your lot, but generally with your position—its duties, its advantages, its dignity). Nor did St. Paul preach without practising; for in the Epistle to the Philippians he avers, "I have learned, in whatsoever state I am, therewith to be content;" and shortly afterward this expression of contentment with his state at the time (*although he was then in captivity*) drops from his pen: "I have all, and abound; I am full." Nor is this great grace of a cheerful acquiescence in the present, whatever it may be, confined to the saints of the Christian Dispensation. Soothing to the heart's natural feverishness is that strain of the Psalmist: "The lines" (the measuring-lines, by which a certain portion of ground is marked out) "are fallen unto me in pleasant places; yea, I have a goodly heritage." And beautiful with a tender beauty is the example of this grace which is given by the Shunammite, who set apart a chamber in her house, with a bed, and a table, and a stool, and a candlestick, for the reception of the Prophet Elisha. In acknowledgment of her good offices, he sent her a message, as if she were a child of this world, desirous of being repaid in this world's coin: "Behold, thou hast been careful for us with all this care, what is to be done for thee? wouldest thou be spoken for to the king, or to the captain of the host?" No! no! Elisha had mistaken the woman. Neither the king nor the commander-in-chief had any thing to offer which was in the smallest degree attractive to such a mind as hers. Scope for quiet cultivation of the domestic affections, and for quiet fulfilment of home duties, was all that she coveted. "She answered, I dwell among mine own people." She dwelt in far Issachar, divided by the whole district of Manasseh from the metropolis of the ten tribes. In that metropolis she would be a stranger, however lifted to eminence, moving in a heartless circle of formalities and (so-called) amusements, for which she had no real taste; experiencing no affection or sympathy from the visitors who thronged her house, nor even from the dependants who waited upon her. So she said—and the words indicate the power which, even under that earlier dispensation, God's grace had gained in her heart—"I dwell among mine own people:" words worthy of a Psalmist, worthy of an Apostle—worthy of him who sung: "The lines are fallen unto me in pleasant places; yea, I have a goodly heritage," and of him who wrote: "I have learned, in whatsoever state I am, therewith to be content." Oh that in an age, when men run to and fro in restless quest of something which at present they have not, when every one, as if by an instinct pervading all classes of society, "wandereth from his place, as a bird wandereth from her nest," we could all reëcho her sentiment, and take it up into our mouths with sincerity: "I dwell among mine own people"—"In my present home I desire to abide, till I exchange it for a better and an eternal one!"

It is not, however, as a beautiful sentiment, but as one of the principles and secrets of a holy life, that we are now advocating the duty of contentment with present things. It is because a cheerful and thankful acquiescence in our present condition is so essential to spiritual progress, that it requires to be pressed so much. We cannot make spiritual progress amid distractions of heart, whether those distractions arise from a melancholy hankering after the past, or from vainly reaching forward to some better and brighter future. And at this point a new line of thought opens itself up in connection with our subject. It is curious and instructive to observe how the Fall has perplexed the original design of our nature, and set the various principles of it at work, each upon an end which is not its own. There is in human nature a principle of rest, which leads us to acquiesce in the present, and a principle of activity and progress, instigating us to further attainments. The principle of rest was meant to operate upon our earthly condition, and to insure contentment with present circumstances. The principle of progress, on the other hand, was meant to operate upon our moral and spiritual attainments, and to urge us on to a higher standard of goodness. But a sad confusion has come in with the Fall, in virtue of which each of these principles works upon that which, in the original design of God, was the end of the other. The principle of rest leads us to acquiesce in a very ordinary standard of moral attainment. We satisfy ourselves entirely with a reputable life and a decorous and devout attention to the externals of religion, more especially if these be united with an accessibility to religious impressions. How quickly and promptly do we, after an access of these impressions, gravitate to the earth again and settle down upon our lees, and develop that tendency toward self-complacent spiritual stagnation, which is so continually the subject of censure in the Holy Scriptures: "Woe to them that are at ease in Zion;" "It shall come to pass at that time, saith the Lord, that I will search Jerusalem with candles, and punish the men that are settled on their lees;" "Thou sayest, I am rich, and increased with goods, and have need of nothing; and knowest not that thou art wretched, and miserable, and poor, and blind, and naked."—On the other hand, the principle of progress concerns itself with our circumstances, our position, and our material welfare. Society in general most energetically improves its condition; and each individual member of it exerts himself to the utmost not to miss his share in the general improvement. In short, if we desired to find words descriptive of the restless progress of our age, and of the aspirations of all, who have imbibed its temper, to be something they are not at present, we could not find words more suitable than those in which St. Paul—even after having sacrificed all things for Christ—describes his own ardent pursuit of the crown and palm-branch, which are held out to the runner in the Christian course: "Brethren, I count not myself to have apprehended; but this one thing I do, forgetting those things which are behind, and reaching forth unto those things which are before, I press toward the mark for the prize." It becomes clear, then, that one thing which we have to do in the pursuit of holiness is to restore (if I may so express it) to their right places and functions the acquiescence and the forward impulse, which there are in our nature; to be easily satisfied as regards our condition, so as not to indulge a wish for the change of it; to be deeply dissatisfied with the little we know of God and of ourselves, and the miserably little we do for Him. Let our whole care be to serve God in the *present* moment of our lives; to taste the peace of the *present* pardon offered to us freely through the Blood of Jesus Christ; to meet faithfully the obligations and responsibilities which the passing hour devolves upon us; to improve to the utmost *present* opportunities either of doing or receiving good. It was said of the manna: "Let no man leave of it until the morning;" and, in like terms, of the Passover Lamb: "Ye shall let nothing remain of it until the morning." Communion with God and a walk in the sunlight of His countenance are like the manna and the Passover Lamb; they are designed for instantaneous enjoyment; they may not be reserved until to-morrow; these viands will not keep until another day.

To-morrow! Another day! How know we that a to-morrow is in store for us? that we shall live to see another day? It is this consideration of the precariousness of life at the best, of its brevity at all events, which, if we could fully grasp it in idea, would make our present worldly condition dwindle down in importance to a mere mathematical point. Very strikingly is this brought out in one of the passages already quoted from St. Paul. He is speaking of the condition of a slave when he writes: "Brethren, let every man, wherein he is called, therein abide with God."

"Art thou called being a servant?" he says, "care not for it" (thy earthly position is a matter of no great moment; do not press or push for a change, *though the change to be pushed for is nothing less than liberty*); "but if thou mayest be made free, use it rather" (if the option of liberty is given you, you need have no hesitation in availing yourself of it [1]).

[1] Unless indeed the *εἰ καὶ* in *εἰ καὶ δύνασαι ἐλεύθερος γενέσθαι* is to be rendered "although" (its usual force). In which case the meaning will be—"nay, although thou mayest be made free,

But how can an exhortation not to be solicitous about a change of position, even when the position is one of bondage in a heathen family, be justified? Such a position would seem at first sight to be fraught with so many drawbacks and disadvantages, even in a moral and spiritual point of view, that the exchange of it for freedom would be worth any exertion, any sacrifice. Doubtless, if it should last any considerable time. But at longest it is to endure only a few short years, and then the Christian slave, who has already been delivered from the servitude of sin, shall be emancipated, not by the rod of the Prætor, but with the glorious liberty of the children of God. And so the Apostle, after bidding Christians "abide with God" in whatsoever condition of life His Providence hath appointed for them, solemnly sums up his argument thus: "But this I say, brethren, the time is short" (literally, *the season*—that remains to us until the coming of the Lord, whether to the world at the second Advent, or to the individual soul at death—*is contracted* into a very brief span). We must work while we have the light. We must redeem the opportunity. As for secular circumstances and position, we must sit loose to them, and not allow them to hold us with too fast a grip. "It remaineth that they that weep be as

use it" (i. e., slavery) "rather." But I cannot help thinking that, if this had been St. Paul's meaning, he would have written rather *ἀλλὰ καὶ εἰ*—"but *even if* thou mayest be made free." The force of *καὶ* is to throw the emphasis on the word immediately succeeding. *'Αλλ' εἰ καὶ δύνασαι*, therefore, may mean, "But if thou *mayest*" (with an emphasis on the *mayest*) "be made free, have thy freedom." It is hard to suppose that St. Paul would have exhorted his converts to prefer slavery to freedom, where the latter might have been had innocently.

though they wept not; and they that rejoice, as though they rejoiced not; and they that buy, as though they possessed not; and they that use this world, as not abusing it: for the fashion of this world passeth away." Hence the comparative unimportance of our worldly position, which may well soothe away any feverish anxiety to change it. All differences of size vanish in the presence of Infinity. All differences of lot vanish in the presence of that tremendous reality, which is called Eternity.

> "Eternity! Eternity!
>   How long art thou, Eternity?
> A moment lasts all joy below,
> Whereby man sinks to endless woe.
> A moment lasts all earthly pain,
> Whereby an endless joy we gain—
>   Ponder, O Man, Eternity."

Strive not, then, for a change of circumstances. Work for God in the present day, as if your horizon were bounded by sunrise and nightfall. How avails it to linger in memory over the past, or to long for the future? The past cannot be recalled or altered. The future (of Time) may never be yours. You are master only of the present.

In concluding the Chapter, let us just advert to another and very different form from that of pressing after mere temporal advancement, in which the restlessness of the present age is manifested. Among the many signs of an unhealthy moral atmosphere now abroad, is a growing discontent with the doctrines and discipline of the Church of our Baptism, of our forefathers. Devout men, catching unawares the infectious desire of the times for progress, crave after something more exciting to the devotional instinct than they conceive the Church of England has to offer. She has not spirituality enough; she chills our fervor with her formality; or, her framework is too stiff, too unaccommodating to emergencies; or, she does not indulge in striking appeals to the imagination and the senses. But I believe that the really spiritual mind, which is bent upon the attainment of Holiness as the one thing needful, while ready, of course, to welcome and adopt all improvements, will not overmuch occupy itself with projects of change, much less will cherish a desire to stray into other Communions, conceived to offer larger helps, or fewer hinderances, to the spiritual life. "Be content with present things," is an excellent precept for religious as well as for worldly dissatisfactions. Surely there is scope enough, material enough, opportunities enough, helps enough, for serving God and benefiting our fellow-creatures, where we are, and under the conditions of our present ecclesiastical system. Rather I should say there is more than enough of all these; for what member or minister of the English Church will say that he has fully availed himself of all the opportunities of gaining or doing good, which the existing system (often complained of as so faulty) gives? How then? Is there something else working at the bottom of the heart, besides a desire to serve God faithfully, and to advance our own salvation, and that of others? Has the mind formed some ideal of a perfect communion here upon the earth, such as never was, never will be, never can be realized in an imperfect and a transitory world? Are we dreaming of perfection in any Church, until the Son of Man sends forth His angels to gather out of His kingdom all scandals, and them that do iniquity? No doubt there is a pleasant excitement in planning and scheming for a brighter and better condition of things. But is not this excitement apt somewhat to distract us from the duties of the present hour, and the one thing needful? The distinctive features of distinct Communions will be all swept away at the Lord's Coming, when unity shall be restored to the Universal Church, and there shall be one flock and one Shepherd; and possibly, long before the Lord's Coming, the keen interest which we personally take in these distinctions shall cease, and we shall be face to face with the realities of Eternity. Then, if we would follow after Holiness, let us not discompose ourselves with any feverish desires for change. Let us say of our ecclesiastical, as well as our temporal position: "I am well where I am. God's Providence has appointed my lot in a Communion, not, it may be, free from defects and weak points (where is such a Communion to be found upon earth?), but certainly Scriptural, and certainly primitive. 'The lines are fallen unto me in pleasant places; yea, I have a goodly heritage.' 'Among my own people,' in the bosom of the Church which brought me to Christ in infancy, will I dwell; and there will I die; and, until I can find a Communion which supplies me with more touching and solemn words for the occasion, I shall determine that the last words read over my remains shall be those of the Office for the Burial of the Dead."

CHAPTER XVII.

THE CENTRIPETAL AND CENTRIFUGAL FORCES OF THE SOUL.

Οὐχὶ πάντες εἰσὶ λειτουργικὰ πνεύματα, εἰς διακονίαν ἀποστελλόμενα διὰ τοὺς μέλλοντας κληρονομεῖν σωτηρίαν; "*Are they not all ministering spirits, sent forth to minister for them who shall be heirs of salvation?*"—HEB. i. 14.

AS a starting-point for the argument of this Chapter, I shall ask my readers to imagine a case which not unfrequently occurs. Let us suppose a good and devout person not to have been called in the order of God's Providence to any regular pursuit—not to have any occupation made ready to his hand. Let us suppose that he needs not to earn a livelihood; that he is born to a position of great affluence, which affluence, however, does not involve the management of real property. And let us further suppose that another equally good man, harassed with overmuch secular work, congratulates him on the abundant leisure for the exercises of devotion, which his circumstances allow. To which the person congratulated replies thus: "It is true, friend, that I have leisure enough (and to spare) for private prayer, the study of the Scriptures, and all other ordinances of Religion;

and that so far my lot is a happy one. But I find myself under a great disadvantage in another respect. I have no occupation, and that is a great drawback. Highly as I esteem, and much as I enjoy, Prayer and the Holy Scriptures, I cannot pray and read the Bible all day long. My mind recoils from an uninterrupted exercise of devotion, and craves for active employment as a necessary ingredient of happiness."

Now, is this recoil of the mind from ceaseless devotion, and its craving after active work, *a disease of the mind, or rather part of the mind's original constitution?* Is it a really natural instinct? or is it a result of the Fall? Few questions can be more important in a practical point of view. For if the desire for active work be a really natural instinct, then the life of unintermitted *exercises* of devotion is a mistake, and the striving after such a life, as pious anchorites and monks have often striven, is a cramping of the mind into an unnatural posture, likely to hinder its free development. But if, on the other hand, this desire for active work connects itself with the sin which is in us, and with the alienation of the human mind from God, which was brought in by the Fall, then no doubt we are furthering the great end of our existence, only when we are engaged in acts of prayer, praise, meditation, or some ordinance of Religion; and any secular pursuit becomes an impertinence as regards the great end of our being.

Now, the passage of Scripture, which stands at the head of the Chapter, seems to answer this question more conclusively than any other. It is true, indeed, that it speaks not of men, but of angels, and therefore seems at first sight to be inapplicable in determining a question of *human* duty. But mind in all rational creatures, whether men or angels, is a thing of the same quality, governed by the same laws, and subjected to the same conditions, although no doubt differing in the clearness of its intuitions, according to the state of existence in which the creature possessed of mind is placed. And in the present instance there is a positive advantage in looking at mind as it exists in Angels, rather than as it exists in men. For the question before us is, whether a certain instinct of the mind, which we all find in ourselves, is a part of the mind's original constitution, or a part of the corruption of our nature. Now, if we looked at ourselves alone, it might not be easy to determine this question. Sin has insinuated itself into all our thoughts and feelings, has given to all of them a certain tinge, so that it might not be easy to say of a particular sentiment how far it is due to the original constitution of our nature, and how far to the sin which has thrown that constitution into disorder. But into the nature of the holy Angels sin never entered; and in them therefore we see mind (or created intelligence) in its really original condition, as it came fresh from the hands of God. And if any man should still demur to our deducing from the study of angelic nature any argument bearing upon human duty, let him consider that Our Lord Himself makes the service which Angels do to God a model of the service which men are bound to do to Him. For it is Our Lord, who has taught us to pray that "God's will may be done upon earth as it is in heaven;" which words surely warrant us in looking to the rational intelligences in heaven—to what the Word of God has revealed, and what the Church of God has received respecting them—as furnishing an example of our own obligations and duties.

What is it, then, which God's Word has revealed to us respecting the pursuits and occupations of Angels? The passage which stands at the head of this Chapter answers the question briefly but exhaustively; and it is most unfortunate that the English translation should here fail (as it fails very seldom indeed) to exhibit the point of the passage. Two radically different Greek words, which call up in the mind associations of an opposite character, are translated by one and the same English word, "minister." "Are they not all *ministering* spirits?"—the word used here is that from which our word "liturgy" comes. It sets before us the Angels as priests of the Heavenly Temple, engaged in the service of praise and adoration. Perhaps the one word, which in English conveys the sense most accurately, is "officiating;" "Are they not all *officiating* spirits?"—"Sent forth to *minister* for them who shall be heirs of salvation." Here the ministration is not the performance of a devotional function, but simply the doing of service. The same word is used where Martha is said to have been cumbered about much *serving;* where the widows of the Hellenists are said to have been neglected in the daily *ministration* (i. e., in the daily distribution of Church funds); and again where the disciples of Antioch are said to have "determined to send relief" (send "for a *ministration*" of temporal resources) "unto the brethren which dwelt in Judea." So that in the life of the holy Angels there is an element of worship and devotion, directed toward God as its object, and an element of active service on behalf of God's children, directed toward man. Excellently are the two discriminated in the Collect for the Festival of St. Michael, in which we pray, that "as God's holy Angels always do Him service in Heaven" (here is the liturgical function of the Angels—their devotional life), "so, by His appointment, they may succor and defend us upon earth" (here is their ministration to man, the business on which God employs them). And with this summary description of their pursuits agrees most entirely every notice we have of them in Holy Scripture. Sometimes they are exhibited to us as engaged in worship, as when, on the birth-night of Christ, they sing the Christmas Anthem, or as when, in the Book of Revelation, they stand round about the throne and cry: "Worthy is the Lamb that was slain to receive power, and riches, and wisdom, and strength, and honor, and glory, and blessing." Sometimes, on the other hand, they visit this lower world upon errands of consolation and succor, as when one of them shot down into the den of lions, and shut the lions' mouths, that they should not hurt Daniel; and another winged his way into St. Peter's prison, and disencumbered him of his chains, and led him forth through bar, and bolt, and sleeping sentinels; and others, more highly favored, ministered refreshment to Our Blessed Lord after His temptation, strengthened and supported Him in His agony, attended on Him at His resurrection, and composed the grave-clothes in so orderly a manner as to refute the stupid and lying report that His sacred body had been stolen; and again at His Ascension addressed a spirit-stirring word to the sorrowing friends who were following Him with their eyes. It would seem that in

Jacob's vision were well symbolized the two functions of Angels. On the grand staircase (for such no doubt it was, and not a ladder with rounds), which the Patriarch saw mounting up with broad steps to Heaven, there were angels of God ascending and descending; some with faces turned to God, as in worship, some with their shining countenances bent downward and their swift feet hastening to the earth, as if intent on the relief of man, "*officiating* spirits, sent forth *on service* in behalf of the heirs of salvation." I have only to add that in the single perfect exemplification of the angelic life upon earth—the life of our sinless Lord and Master—constant exercises of devotion went hand in hand with constant relief of man's necessities. He followed up nights of Prayer by days of toil in the service of the ignorant and the suffering.

In the light of these observations let us look again at the case supposed at the beginning of the Chapter. The question which was raised in connection with that case is now solved. *There is no sin in that instinctive desire of external activity, which we find in ourselves*—in that necessity for a definite pursuit which all feel, and which those who are without regular employment feel painfully. This desire is part of the original constitution of our mind, not part of its acquired depravity. There seem to be two tendencies in the original constitution of every upright intelligence. I may illustrate them by a reference to those forces of the material universe, which are called centripetal and centrifugal. What is it which causes the rotation of a planet round the sun? First, there must have been the primary impulse given to it by the hand of the Creator, when it was first formed and driven forth into space. But if this were the only impulse upon the planet, it would simply travel ever farther and farther from the point whence it started, coming into collision, perhaps, with other similar bodies on its erratic course. But another force, continually pressing upon it, binds it to a centre, and keeps it in an orderly revolution. Launched into space, it is caught by the attraction of that enormous body, the sun, which never ceases for an instant to act upon it. It sweeps through space still in obedience to its primary impulse, which indeed alone preserves it from falling into the sun; but the power of gravitation confines it to its orbit. Now, in the moral and mental constitution of each one of us there is something similar to this arrangement of the material universe. We are made each one of us for work, for a certain sphere of service; we are qualified for this sphere by certain abilities, and sent into a fallen world, where there are a thousand things to be done, in retrieving the effects of the Fall, in re-establishing order, in assuaging sorrow, in enlightening ignorance, in removing sin; and where also there is (at least among all civilized people) an organization of society, involving a division of labor and a great variety of pursuits. Be the work allotted to us by Providence what it may—be it in itself even dry and repelling—the mind can create an interest in it, by simply throwing itself into what has to be done. But then this throwing his mind into a pursuit is not the *sole* condition of a man's happiness. We feel that it is not, whenever our pursuit wearies our spirits, whenever we commit ourselves, without an attempt at self-control, to the interest of the hour, whatever that may be. We soon come to the bottom of any interest, however high and pure it may be, whether it be an interest in Science, or in Literature, or, better still, in a philanthropic scheme. Our interests are something like our horses, very pleasant to ride while they are fresh, but wearing and wearying to their riders when they are overridden. And why is this, but because there is another condition of man's happiness, over and above the having a pursuit? The soul, in order to be holy and happy (they are only two sides of the same thing), must be continually drawn in toward its centre. Now, God is the centre of the soul, who alone can satisfy all its aspirations after light, and truth, and good. This bias of the soul toward God, this profound gnawing feeling of unrest out of Him, is the soul's centripetal force, just as the craving after work is its centrifugal force. And the due operation of both the forces together, the recognition of God while we are busily engaged in the work which He has given us to do, the turning toward Him in heart while our hands are executing His tasks, or our feet speeding on His errands, this is the path taken by the mind, when obedient, not indeed to the law of the Fall, but to the impulses given it at its Creation. It is an orderly path, and therefore a peaceful and happy path, the only path which can (I do not say gratify, but) satisfy and content the spirit.

But then observe that, in order fully to realize the effect, there must be an interlacing of the recognition of God with our business, not a separation of the two. There is many a Christian who reaches nothing more than this (nay, who aims at nothing more), that devotion shall have its little hour in the day, and business its long hours; and great is his complacency, if the business hours are not allowed to trench upon the hour of devotion. I am not saying any thing against stated periods of devotion; they are absolutely essential, and it is only too certain that in the absence of stated periods the spirit of devotion would evaporate altogether. But I am saying that the soul will never taste a full satisfaction, nor travel in its appointed orbit, until it has learned more or less (using ejaculatory prayer as its instrument) to mix devotion with work. The planet does not at one time travel in obedience to the centrifugal, and then again in obedience to the centripetal force; but at every moment of time both forces are acting upon it, the one speeding it on its course, the other drawing it in toward the sun. The soul must not leave God for an instant, if it is to be perfectly joyous and contented. Let it take but a step away from Him, and it is at once in a region of excitement and unrest, and so far forth of danger. The condition of the soul, when in its orbit, is well represented by these words of Hele's Devotions, which have often struck me as singularly beautiful and edifying: "Grant that I may walk before Thee in a constant awe of Thy sacred Presence, and in such a devout and heavenly frame of mind, as may lead me to be frequently lifting up my heart to Thee, in acts of adoration and thanksgiving, of resignation and dependence." Remember that the New Testament Prayer Precept makes *unbroken* communion with God obligatory upon us. It names no seasons for prayer, or rather, it names every season: "Pray without ceasing."

My reader, I do not ask whether you have completely acquired the habit of interpenetrating your daily employments with the spirit of devotion (that is the case with none of us, least of all probably with the present writer); but are you placing this before you as your standard, and sincerely trying to reach it? Ejaculatory prayer is the great means of reaching it. Do you ever use ejaculatory prayer? Do you ever lift up your heart to God in the midst of your work, praying Him to shield you from temptation, to bless you in what you are doing, and, at all events, not to let you wander very far from His side? Do not say it is impossible; for to this and no lower standard you are called, both by the constitution of your nature, and by the precept, "Pray without ceasing;" and by the grace of God all things which He commands are possible. You will say, perhaps, "I try to keep my mind continually in the right track; but alas! it is thrown off its balance a thousand times a day, by having to do things in a hurry and against time; by a warm conversation; by a piece of interesting news; by domestic worries and cares; by little rubs of the temper." So it is most truly. The mind wants steadying and setting right many times a day. It resembles a compass placed on a rickety table; the least stir of the table makes the needle swing round and point untrue. Let it settle, then, till it points aright. Be perfectly silent for a few moments, thinking of Jesus; there is an almost divine force in silence. Drop the thing that worries, that excites, that interests, that thwarts you; let it fall, like a sediment, to the bottom, until the soul is no longer turbid; and say secretly: "Grant, I beseech Thee, merciful Lord, to thy faithful servant pardon and peace; that I may be cleansed from all my sins, and serve Thee with a *quiet mind.*"

Yes! with a quiet mind. We cannot serve Him with a turbid one; it is a mere impossibility. Thus composing ourselves from time to time, thus praying, and setting the mind's needle true, we shall little by little approximate toward that devout frame, which binds the soul to its true centre, even while it travels through worldly business, worldly excitements, worldly cares.

CHAPTER XVIII.

OF THE NECESSITY OF AN OCCUPATION, AND OF THE RIGHT WAY OF PURSUING IT.

"*Because he was of the same craft, he abode with them, and wrought: for by their occupation they were tent-makers.*"—ACTS xviii. 3.

ST. PAUL, like every other minister of Christ's Gospel, had a right to receive support from the persons to whom he ministered. But there were good reasons why he did not see fit to avail himself of this right. In the first place, he wished to make himself an example of quiet industry to his converts. Some of them, who wanted mental ballast, had been unduly excited and thrown out of the groove of their ordinary pursuits by the revelations of Christianity, and by the influences which the Gospel brought to bear upon them; it would calm and sober them, and help to bring them back to a regular life, if they saw their Apostle, a man who had been favored with the most extraordinary revelations, "caught away as far as the third heaven," "caught away[1] into Paradise,"

[1] Our version "caught *up*" is in both cases inaccurate. There is no preposition to represent "up." The words are ἁρπαγέντα . . . ἡρπάγη. An upward direction may be *implied* in the case of "the third heaven;" but in that of "Paradise," not so. For

earning his bread by laboring at a common handicraft in the intervals of his ministry. Again: he was pleased to be able to feel that his preaching was gratuitous, which it could not have been had he accepted payment for it. It was a satisfaction to know that, in earning his bread by a trade, rather than by his ministry, he was doing something more than he was strictly bound to do, something which he might have left undone without sin. Again, the having a trade gave him scope for the exercise of two most important Christian graces, Self-denial and Almsgiving. The extra work and weariness, which the trade entailed, was a means of keeping under his body and bringing it into subjection; while the money which it brought in to him was employed in relieving the wants of others as well as his own; for he says to the elders of Ephesus: "Yea, ye yourselves know, that these hands have ministered unto my necessities, and *to them that were with me.* I have showed you all things, how that *so laboring ye ought to support the weak*, and to remember the words of the Lord Jesus, how He said, It is more blessed to give than to receive." So St. Paul, impelled by these motives, as also, doubtless, by the example of his Divine Master, who up to the age of thirty had followed the trade of a carpenter, "making" (as Justin Martyr informs us) "ploughs and yokes for oxen"—St. Paul, joining himself in partnership with Aquila and Priscilla, became a manufacturer of hair-cloth or leather tents, having learned that trade in his youth, according to the wise maxim of the Jewish

"Paradise" is the place of departed spirits, conceived of by the Jews as in the centre (or heart) of the earth.

Rabbis, who said that every boy should be taught a trade, upon which he might fall back for a maintenance, in case of necessity.

The Apostle no doubt found his account in his trade, though it imposed upon him toils and cares, which to a spirit less ardent than his might have seemed superfluous. Independently of the conscious security which there was in the self-denial of such a course, independently also of the blessedness of giving for the relief of others, which his trade enabled him to taste, there must have been a ballast given to his mind by work, very necessary to steady it when it was rocked (as it often was) by strong emotions, or lifted up to high contemplations. And it should be remarked that the work, being a handicraft, left his mind comparatively free for prayer and meditation, with which it cannot be doubted that he was continually feeding it. One can imagine that God would often visit him in his work with high and elevating, and even entrancing thoughts, which would more than compensate for the bodily weariness it must have entailed. This would have been quite in accordance with the usual plan on which Divine visions and Divine calls are vouchsafed. Gideon, threshing wheat by the wine-press, is greeted by an angel of the Lord. Elisha's path, as he ploughs with twelve yoke of oxen, is crossed by Elijah, who throws his mantle upon him. David is tending the sheep, when he is fetched out of the field to be anointed and saluted king. Matthew, as he pores over his accounts, and enters in his books the payments made to him at his office, is called to be an Apostle. Peter, as he draws his net to shore, has a manifestation made to him of the Divine power, which brings him to the Saviour's knees. On the eyes of the wise men, as they gaze upon the starry heavens, dawns the star of Bethlehem, which announces the Saviour's birth. And possibly, as St. Paul was stitching together the goat's-hair, which was the material of his trade, the slight and temporary nature of the habitations he was manufacturing may have crossed him, and then there may have come sweeping across his mind grand thoughts of the fleeting nature of the body, which is the soul's tent, and of the durable mansion which God will provide for the spirit hereafter; thoughts such as he expresses in that most solemn passage of one of his Epistles: "For we know that if our earthly house of this tabernacle" (literally, "of the tent") "were dissolved, we have a building of God, an house not made with hands, eternal in the heavens."

In our last Chapter we saw that there are two forces in the soul of man, standing quite independent of the sin that is in him, and which we ventured to call the centrifugal and centripetal forces of the soul, the one driving him into the outer world, and urging him to active work in the path of duty, the other drawing him in, even while he so works, toward God, who is the soul's true centre of repose. Having paid some attention in the earlier part of the work to the latter of these two forces; having spoken at some length on the contemplation of God, on faith in God, on the love of God—we will dilate briefly in this Chapter on the other force, which drives the mind into things external, and corresponds to the impulse given to planets at their creation, in virtue of which they travel on their appointed paths. Consider, then, the necessity to Holiness, and therefore to happiness, of an outward *occupation:* "He abode with them and *wrought:* for by *their occupation* they were tent-makers."

Let us see what hints, likely to be practically useful in the pursuit of Holiness, can be given on this subject.

Of course, for the larger class of people there is an occupation made ready to their hands. Most men—all but the few who are born to independence—have a pursuit (a profession or a trade) by which they earn their livelihood. Their own leanings, or the destination of their parents, or circumstances over which they have had no control—anyhow, the Providence of God, by some of its manifold drawings—has assigned to them this line of life, with the particular duties involved in it. The chief advice, then, that is needed here is how to draw into spiritual account, and to make available for the purposes of the spiritual life, that task which is of daily recurrence and obligation. And in order to this, let it be firmly settled in the mind, before we put our hand to our work, and let us suffer the mind from time to time to revert to the thought, that what we are about to do is the task assigned to us in the order of God's Providence, that it is a task which He will inspect, and that it must be executed as well as ever we are able, in order that it may meet His approval. There are children, who are too young to be left alone in the preparation of their lessons. The teacher must sit with them, while they prepare; they must work under his eye, and have him by them to apply to and ask help from, when they come across a difficulty. Now, some of the deepest lessons of Divine Truth are to be learned from our management of children; and the way of so doing work, as that it may be a source of spiritual consolation and strength, is among these lessons. Do the work under the eye of your Heavenly Master; and look up in His face from time to time for His help and blessing: an internal colloquy with Him ever and anon, so far from being a distraction, will be a furtherance. For no work can in any high sense prosper, which is not done with a bright, elastic spirit; and there is no means of keeping the spirit bright and elastic but by keeping it near to God. Another point is, never to allow ourselves to think of our work as a distraction or a hinderance to piety. Regard it in its true light, morally and spiritually. Think of it as contributing to healthfulness and cheerfulness of mind, as a steadying and sobering influence, preventing those extravagances into which without it the mind might run. Remember also how often in the Scriptures God has come across simple men in the way of their daily task—come across them miraculously in the instances cited above—but He is as ready to meet them now on the field of commonplace occupations, in the ordinary methods of His Providence and His Grace. Do but keep as close under His eye, when working, as you can contrive to do, and open your heart to Him as often as you can; and you shall doubtless hear His whispers in your conscience, and experience the instilment of some good and elevating thought into your mind. But the most important point of advice in an age like ours, when men in all conditions of life are overweighted with work, and in a country like ours, whose inhabitants are so little meditative and so constitutionally busy, is to aim rather at doing well what we do, than at getting through much. Francis of Sales thought that the great bane of the spiritual life in most men is that eagerness and undue activity of the natural mind, which leads to precipitancy and hurry. He states his case too strongly, as all men are apt to do, who think they have got hold of an important secret; but there is valuable truth in what he says. Hurry—the struggle to get through a great deal in a short time, as every one is naturally prompted to do, who finds his table covered with correspondence as thick as a field in the Polar regions with snow, and feels that without an extraordinary effort to-morrow's duties will come crowding in on the heels of today's work—is very prejudicial to our moral and spiritual well-being. The eager impulsiveness to wipe away work, and get well rid of it, is not a temper in which spiritual progress can be made. It was the snare into which Martha fell, who allowed herself to be "cumbered about much serving:" she might have served, and it was necessary and proper that she should serve; but it was neither necessary nor proper to "be cumbered." The Apostle enjoins that we shall "not" be "slothful in business, but fervent in spirit, serving the Lord." "Not slothful in business"—that is, not lazy, while busy. But is not this a contradiction in terms? How can a man be lazy while he is busy? The experience of every much-occupied man furnishes a ready answer. We may be *spiritually* lazy while busy, and by being so may let all our work run to waste, as regards any real fruit of it. To work with a fidgety, anxious, uneasy mind, not setting God before us while we work, but thinking only of the hundred-and-one other calls, which we have to meet as soon as this is satisfied—this it is to be lazy while we are busy. Surely a vast number of people in the present day know what this temper of mind is. And what is the remedy? The remedy is to recommend the work to God, and humbly ask His blessing and His aid, as we may do with the utmost confidence, if the work be really that which His Providence has assigned to us; then, resolutely to refuse to attend to more than one thing at a time, and to let every thing else drop, till that one thing is done. Other things must wait. Some of them we shall be able probably to do by-and-by. Not a few of them will do themselves. And some of them, maybe, we shall have to leave undone. Let us not be disquieted. If the spirit of the doer have been right, all will be well. And the right spirit is not one that is "careful and troubled about many things," but collected, calm, fervent, angelical. Is not God's will to be done in earth, as it is in heaven? And can we imagine distraction, or precipitancy, or restless impulsiveness among the angels in heaven? The devotional writer already referred to says admirably well: "Rivers which glide peaceably through the valleys bear great boats and rich merchandise; and the rain which falls gently on the fields makes them fruitful in grass and corn; but torrents and rivers which run rapidly ruin the bordering country, and are unprofitable for traffic; and vehement and tempestuous rains furrow the fields. Never was work well done with too much violence and earnestness." So much for the method in which we should strive to execute the work of our calling.—But, in very many (if not absolutely in all) pursuits, there are leisure moments and occasional intermissions. Those who nourish a high spiritual ambition will endeavor to turn these also to spiritual account. They will feel that just as a necessity to preach the Gospel was laid upon St. Paul, a necessity which he could in nowise escape from, so our ordinary pursuit, whatever it be, is made obligatory upon us by the imperative demand of our daily wants. However devoutly we may work, we are working for ourselves, when we follow our trade or our profession; for it is by this craft that we have our wealth. But in our leisure moments it is open to us to do something gratuitously for the cause of Christ—either in one form or other to give labor to His cause, or by extra work to procure the means of furthering it. This is what St. Paul did. Though the care of all the Churches devolved upon him daily, and the due discharge of his ministry must have been, one would think, more than sufficient to engross his every leisure moment, yet he took up again the trade which he had learned in his youth, though he was under no obligation whatever to do so, and thus had the deep satisfaction of feeling that in his ministry he was working unpaid for the Master, whose free grace had done every thing for him. Truly a sublime and heroic generosity; and one which, at however long a distance, it is possible for modern Christians to imitate. There are many fields of Church work, in all of which labor and money are sorely needed. Might not the professional man, might not the tradesman, give labor (either personal or remunerative) in one of these fields? Is there nothing which we might do for the cause of Christ, if so disposed, in leisure hours? This answer will rise to the lips of many readers: "My regular work puts such a strain upon me, that I find myself fit for nothing—more dead than alive at the end of the day." Doubtless it may be so. And probably our overwrought modern civilization, habituating generation after generation, as it does, to softness of life, has enfeebled the constitutions of all of us, and made us less equal to hardships than were men of old. Still we must not blink the great fact that a more responsible and more anxious occupation than St. Paul's never yet fell to any man's lot; and yet that he found time, by honest industry, to earn enough to support himself and relieve the wants of those around him. Probably, if we could do our work in a brighter and less anxious spirit, it would wear us less. It is worry, not work, that wears. And then, in the case of our undertaking, in our leisure moments, some gratuitous Church work—be it school teaching, or District visiting, or mere extra labor to earn money for charities—there would always be the thought of *its being gratuitous* to uphold us, and a feeling also of security, from the circumstance of self-denial, which we are at all times so prone to evade, being wrought into the plan and texture of our life.

I have spoken of cases (and these are, at least among men, the great majority) where persons have a definite occupation, a line of life marked out for them in the way of a trade or a profession. But what shall we say of those who are not called upon to work for a livelihood, and whose only regular business is the administration of a property or of a household, which, while it may be under certain circumstances heavy, may also be so light as to allow long intervals of leisure? Is not reading, it might be said, the suitable occupation for such people? For reading, if intelligently pursued, is a means of cultivating the mind and of self-improvement, which doubtless should be one great object with all thoughtful and earnest persons. But surely mere reading, without any outcome of the study in the shape of writing or teaching, hardly constitutes by itself such an occupation as the Christian mind craves after. It is hardly suitable that, in a world full of ignorance, misery, and sin, and where the ignorance, misery, and sin, may be greatly relieved by our faithful and pious endeavors, a man or woman should wrap themselves up even in the improvement of their own minds. Let us be quite sure that, in all such cases, some definite work, with a definite bearing on the physical, intellectual, or moral good of our fellow-creatures, is an essential to Holiness, and to that inward joy and peace which is the very element of Holiness. As I said above, there is no lack nowadays of posts of usefulness; the lack is of persons to fill them. There is a large field of Church work open to us at home and abroad—rough work much of it, disheartening work much of it, and therefore manifesting only the more principle in those who take it up and carry it on. Let every unoccupied Christian choose one of these fields of labor, determining which it shall be by the little pointings of God's finger in Providence, and by the direction in which his instincts, powers, and capacities, lead him. We read in the Scriptures of whole households taking on them some one department of Church work, giving *point* to their efforts by devoting themselves to one, and *consistency* by the combination of the various members of the family—"Ye know the house of Stephanas, that it is the first-fruits of Achaia, and that they have addicted themselves to the ministry of the saints," to some service for the saints—perhaps to the exercise of hospitality. Why should it not be so now? Circumstances no doubt are widely different, and must modify the form of the service; but the principle that each Christian should do what in him lies to further the great work of the Christian Church can never pass away, however various its applications may be.

Finally, I must give a rather fuller development to a thought which has been brought before us in the prosecution of our argument—the advantage which in one important respect manual work has over mental. It is analogous to the advantage which generally, in spiritual matters, the poor and ignorant have over the rich and cultivated. It is the spirit, or rational faculty, with which God, who is a Spirit, must be served. That the outward pursuit, then, should make as little demand upon the mind as possible, that the inner man should be left as free as possible to turn toward God at any moment, is an advantage of which a devout soul may avail itself. St. Paul's thoughts doubtless were often with his Master, while he was making his tents. And those who covet above all things a closer communion with God, will assuredly think no scorn of an occupation which engages the hands rather than the thinking faculty. Doubtless intellectual pursuits are, in the order of things, nobler than a common handicraft. But there is "a spirit," as well as a mind, in man. And if a handicraft gives greater scope for the action of the spirit—if the husbandman as he digs his field, the lace-woman as she plies her bobbins, the shepherd as he tends his flock, nay, the boy set to keep the birds from the crop, are at least free to feed their spirits the while with the thought of God's power, wisdom, and goodness, they are more than compensated for their intellectual loss by their spiritual gain, and they find consolation and refreshment in place of the weariness of merely mental effort—a weariness thus commented upon, in accents of bitter disappointment, by the wisest of men: "Of making many books there is no end; and much study is a weariness of the flesh."

CHAPTER XIX.

SELF-SACRIFICE A TEST OF THE LOVE OF GOD.

"*And when He was gone forth into the way, there came one running, and kneeled to Him, and asked Him, Good Master, what shall I do that I may inherit eternal life? And Jesus said unto him, Why callest thou Me good? there is none good but One, that is, God. Thou knowest the commandments, Do not commit adultery, Do not kill, Do not steal, Do not bear false witness, Defraud not, Honor thy father and mother. And he answered and said unto Him, Master, all these have I observed from my youth. Then Jesus beholding him loved him, and said unto him, One thing thou lackest: go thy way, sell whatsoever thou hast, and give to the poor, and thou shalt have treasure in heaven: and come, take up the cross, and follow Me.*"—MARK x. 17–21.

OUR subject in this little treatise is the pursuit of Holiness. Now, the spring and motive of all Holiness being the love of God, we have enlarged upon this grand topic in several of the Chapters, and have spoken much of the beauty and blessedness of the Divine character, as having a tendency to attract toward God the hearts of men. But the general complexion of the subject, and the tenor of our remarks upon it, have made it quite necessary, in bringing our argument to a close, to say one or two words of solemn warning. It is very easy to delude ourselves into the notion that we have the love of God, and are under its influence. It is easy at all times to mistake a sentiment for a principle, a transient feeling for a deeply-rooted affection. And therefore the Holy Scriptures, which aim at implanting and nourishing, not sentiments but principles, while they supply us in the Psalms with aspirations after God, which can only proceed from genuine love, and while they set forth everywhere the beauty and attractiveness of His character, are careful to furnish practical tests of a very stringent kind, whereby we may try our hearts and ascertain how far they are really under the empire of God's love. One of these tests I shall consider on the present occasion, reserving another for the following Chapter.

The interview of the rich young man with Our Lord is one of those many incidents, which derive importance from being recorded three times in the New Testament. There are few passages of Scripture the teaching of which is more apt to be misunderstood. The key to it is to be found in the circumstances of the young man, and in what transpires of his character. He was "very rich," "had great possessions;" his circumstances, therefore, gave him no trouble; he never knew what it was to be straitened. He was "young;" and therefore we may assume that he was in health, and had all that bright sanguineness and energy which only health can give. He was "a ruler," possibly the president of some synagogue, one therefore for whom his position gave a sort of guarantee that he was a man of virtue and piety. And to a great extent he really was so. He had observed, at least in the letter, the commandments of the second Table; and that his observance of them was, so far as it went, commendable, and had really proceeded from a principle of duty, we may gather from the circumstance that, when he mentioned it, Our Lord seems to have smiled on him in approbation: "Then Jesus beholding him loved him." It was not in a Pharisaic spirit of pride that he said, "Master, all these have I observed from my youth." What he desired was, that this great Teacher of Divine Truth who had appeared in Israel should point out to him some arduous attainment of virtue, some one great moral effort, more arduous than the commandments of the second Table (which he does not seem to have understood in their spiritual import), by which he might secure the prize which he professed to covet—"eternal life."

Now, here was a man—fair and promising in many points (may we not call him a man of *great* spiritual promise?)—whom Our Lord was about to test by the application to his conscience of the first and great commandment in a practical form. For that this is the true significance of Christ's dealing with him cannot be doubted. It is very observable how the only commandments, which are specified to this young man as the pathway to eternal life, are those of the second Table. Why is this? It is impossible to suppose that Our Lord, in bringing the Law to bear upon his conscience, would omit the commandment which *He Himself called the first and great commandment:* "Thou shalt love the Lord thy God with all thy heart, and with all thy soul, and with all thy mind." Assuredly He does not omit it; but makes it here, as He did on other occasions, the most important point of all. But He begins with the lower and less arduous, before He comes to the higher and more arduous, requirements of the Law, as if He had said to the rich young man: "Tell me first how you have loved your neighbor, whom you have seen, before I proceed to inquire how you love God, whom you have not seen." The young man's answer virtually is: "I have from my earliest youth fulfilled my duty to my neighbor." "Assuming that you have done so, for argument's sake," Our Lord continues, "how do you stand disposed toward God? Is your heart right with Him? Is it *whole* with Him, as a heart must be, if it is to be right?" This is the import of Our Lord's words; but He does not put the question thus explicitly. Doubtless, if He had done so, the young man's conscience would have evaded it. The pressing of the love of God in an abstract form gives great room, as I observed at the opening of the Chapter, for self-deception. And especially is this the case, when the persons, on whom it is pressed, are free from trouble in their circumstances and in their bodily frame. When the sun of prosperity shines out warm and bright upon us; when we are in a state of robust health, and have a flow of animal spirits; when our friends are around us, our homes happy, our means abundant for our needs, and there is no call for pinching, or saving, or straitening; when, moreover, our reputation is good, and we are looked up to in the little circle in which we move—nothing is easier, under these circumstances, than to feel an occasional glow of gratitude to the Giver of all these blessings, and to mistake that for the love which is the fulfilling of the first and great commandment. So, without mentioning, or even suggesting, to this young man the love of God, Our Lord proposes to him a practical test, whereby it shall be made evident how far he is under the influence of that love. He bids him sell all that he has, distribute it among the poor, and, embracing the hardship and contempt to which Christ's earliest followers exposed themselves, attach himself to the little company of disciples, who went about the country in attendance upon their Divine Master. Just as some chemical test thrown into a colorless liquid immediately turns it blue, and detects the presence of steel, so this test applied to the young man's heart and character, in which hitherto there had seemed to be such brave spiritual promise, clouded it all over, and detected in it what Our Lord afterward calls a "trust in riches." By a trust in riches is meant, not a trust in riches to save the soul, *according to the vulgar conception of salvation* (nobody attributes to riches any such power), but a trust in riches to content and satisfy the heart. Now, this trust is inconsistent with the love of God. For just as love among men, love as it exists between the sexes, involves a longing for the company of the person loved, a great complacency in that company, a readiness to do any thing and every thing to win that person's favor, and *a contempt of every thing else in comparison of that person's smile;* so the love of God involves supreme delight in Him, contemplation of His beauty and His excellency, enjoyment of communion with Him in that relation to Himself, into which He has been pleased to bring us, and *a counting of all things but loss, so we may but win His favor and approval.* It is the uniform characteristic of true love to delight in making sacrifices, when called upon by its object to do so. Now, God, by the mouth of Christ, called this young man to do what the earlier Apostles had done, and what St. Paul afterward did, "to suffer the loss of all things, and to count them but dung, so as he might win" God's favor and acceptance. The man had recognized Christ, not indeed as the God-man or the Saviour of the world, but as a teacher sent from God, by coming to inquire of Him the way of eternal life. "The blessedness of eternal life"—this is the scope of Our Lord's answer to him—"consists in such a supreme delight in God as makes us disrelish, by comparison, every pleasure which life and the world have to offer. Now, therefore, I, as a teacher sent by God and speaking His words, and as recognized by you in that capacity, require you to show that you take this supreme delight in God, in the same way as Peter here and the rest have done, by just dropping those earthly possessions which you hold so tightly in your grip, and, with hands and arms thus liberated, embracing God as your chief good."

Such is the real significance of the story, which is very liable, however, to be misread. We shall misread it entirely, if we suppose that Our Lord recommends the renunciation of property as *a work of extraordinary merit, which, when once done, will secure eternal life to the doer of it.* Many monks, it is to be feared, have fallen into this misapprehension of Christ's meaning, and, after having parted with all their worldly goods, and assumed the monastic habit, have not found themselves nearer to "eternal life" than they were before. They ought to have noticed and heeded the closing words of the recommendation: "Take up thy cross, and follow Me." It is not simply an abandonment, but *an abandonment which is to pave the way for a new pursuit and interest*, that is recommended. As I have phrased it above, it is not a mere dropping of the goods, which Christ requires, but a dropping of these in order to embrace God—God's kingdom, God's righteousness, God's will.

He does not require from us an exactly similar abandonment of all that we possess. But two demands, of a kindred character, there can be no doubt He does make upon every soul to whom His Gospel comes. First: we must actually and literally drop *something*, not only of our worldly substance, but of the comforts and blessings, whatever they be, which make life enjoyable to us, as a testimony that at His bidding we are ready to resign the whole. It was to His disciples for all time, not to an individual, whose case might require a special treatment, that He said: "Sell that ye have, and give alms; provide yourselves bags which wax not old, a treasure in the heavens that faileth not, where no thief approacheth, neither moth corrupteth. For where your treasure is, there will your heart be also." Moreover, by the example of His Apostle, almost more cogently than by any precept, He enjoins that we shall "keep under our bodies and bring them into subjection," and that we shall never use our Christian liberty to the full extent. —In the second place: we are required to drop absolutely and at once all *trust* in riches, that is, all such affection to earthly and created good as leads us to place in it the contentment and satisfaction of our souls. "Lay up for yourselves treasures in heaven." "Seek those things which are above, where Christ sitteth on the right hand of God. Set your affection on things above, not on things on the earth. For ye are dead, and your life is hid with Christ in God." We must maintain, toward the comforts and blessings of this life, such an attitude of mind as would make us quite ready to strip ourselves bare of them, should God require us to do so. And it is vain to hope that this can be done without actual mortification and self-denial. To the precept just quoted, "Set your affection on things above, not on things on the earth," is immediately subjoined, as a necessary condition of heavenly-mindedness, "*Mortify therefore your members which are upon the earth.*" Where there is no endurance of hardness as a good soldier of Jesus Christ, there the love of God and of Christ is apt to degenerate into a mere sentiment, exerting no power over the will, and deluding the heart by a vain show of piety. As to the mode, therefore, of exercising this mortification, and maintaining the spirituality of it, I will give a few counsels.

First: it should be deeply considered what it is that has to be mortified in us—that it is *the affection to created good*, not in one particular shape, but *in all its forms.* We may not be coveting or striving after a fortune (that is, after a superfluous amount of this world's wealth), and yet it is quite possible that our hearts may be set upon the world, and that we may be looking to God's creatures, rather than to communion with Himself, to fill and content the soul. The amiable, estimable, unambitious man, who has no notion of aspiring to eminence or rising in life, may yet be warmly attached to created good. Nor need it be created good in one only form. The Paradise of the majority of men has several ingredients in it; but all the ingredients are of the earth, earthy. The first of these ingredients is a comfortable competence—not more. The next is good health, or, at all events, health good enough for the enjoyment of life. Then comes the being surrounded by relations and friends—the sympathies and charities of the domestic hearth. If the man is at all highly cultivated, some intellectual stimulus, literature in some cases, politics in others, enters into the idea of a satisfactory life. With almost all, some definite and useful occupation during the better part of the day is felt to be an essential constituent of happiness. Then also respectability—a certain amount of human esteem—is a *sine quâ non.* Surely there is many and many a soul, which secretly whispers to itself: "Give me all these things, and I shall need nothing more. If these conditions were only made permanent, I could live on earth forever, and should seek for nothing better." And it must be added that the larger is the share of these things which falls to our lot, the greater is the risk of our becoming dangerously attached to them. Our hearts are constantly throwing out suckers of affection; and whatsoever support these suckers find in the neighborhood, they will infallibly twine themselves round it and creep over it. And, that the heart's affections should be allowed to cleave to any earthly object or objects exclusively, so that its thoughts, desires, hopes, should all be wrapped up in that object or objects, this is the love of the world or of the creature, even should the mind be a stranger to what is called covetousness and ambition. The first step, therefore, to be taken by him who would exercise a wise mortification, is to consider deeply in what form or forms of earthly good he is naturally disposed to place his happiness. What forms yield him, constituted as he is, most comfort, most gratification? Is it the sympathy of friends and relations? Is it human esteem? Is it a luxurious ease, a career free from serious troubles and annoyances—that life should flow on in an unbroken tenor, without anxiety and pressure? Is it the gratification of ambition, the coming successfully out of the struggles of life? Is it amusement and recreation? Whatever it be, there let him exercise a jealous watchfulness over himself; there let him mortify his will. To mortify the will is often a far greater cross than to inflict the severest penance on the body. There let him lay by force restrictions upon himself, sometimes sharply refusing all indulgence to the propensity, however in itself innocent, never at any time giving it too free a rein. In giving this counsel, I am only exhibiting the principle upon which all true mortification must proceed, not disparaging the two specially recognized forms of it, Fasting and Almsgiving. These are chosen by the Word of God with great wisdom, as involving self-denial in respect of those temptations which offer most attraction to the mass of mankind—"the lust of the flesh, the lust of the eyes, and the pride of life." We are all under the dominion, more or less, of our senses; and therefore Fasting, if not always in the shape of total abstinence, yet in that of spare diet at certain seasons, and of habitual self-control, is for all of us more or less of a necessary discipline. Again: we are all apt to cling to and to wrap ourselves in the comforts of this life; and, therefore, a free flinging abroad among the distressed of the money which represents these comforts, a liberal parting with our substance for works of piety or charity, a stripping of ourselves of all superfluities, lest the mere sight of abundance should tempt us to that fatal whisper, "Soul, thou hast much goods laid up for many years; take thine ease, eat, drink, and be merry"—this also is a form of self-denial to which all, according to their means, are bound. And, if there were but a stronger conviction upon our minds of the reality and nearness of unseen things, if the world to come and the revelations of the Gospel were no mere phantoms to us, flitting before the eye of the imagination, but truths grasped by us with the hand of a living faith, a corresponding disparagement of worldly possessions, exactly proportioned in its strength to the strength of the conviction, would, as a necessary consequence, take possession of the soul. It was so, when man, by the earliest operations of the Holy Ghost, first began to experience, with a vividness which has since been rarely exhibited, "the powers of the world to come." Immediately after Pentecost, there was a bright gleam of sunshine in the Church's history, which, for the moment, made the gaunt form of poverty vanish like a ghost at cockcrow: "Neither was there among them any that lacked; for as many as were possessors of lands or houses sold them, and brought the prices of the things that were sold, and laid them down at the Apostles' feet; and distribution was made unto every man according as he had need." The result was natural and necessary. The more intensely a man realizes unseen and eternal things, the more he can afford to dispense with the things that are seen and are temporal.

But, finally, in order to maintain the spirituality

of acts of mortification, it is necessary to regard them as standing in the closest connection with the love of God and with delight in communion with Him, in short, *as being only the negative form of this love and delight.* Mortification which should terminate upon itself would be of little or no value. God has treasure in store for us, even "such good things as pass man's understanding;" and it is only in order to our more vivid appreciation and keener relish for this heavenly treasure that He requires us to disencumber ourselves of the earthly. It is only in order that we may bask in His sunlight, may be fanned by His breezes, may walk abroad among His landscapes, may lift up our eyes to His stars, that He invites us to come out of the narrow house of earthly comfort, and turn our backs upon the false artificial lights which are kindled there. *Mortification is not an end in itself; it is but a means to an end*—that end being the springing up in our hearts of a fountain of eternal joy. And therefore to cultivate a taste for spiritual enjoyments, and to place one's contentment and satisfaction more and more exclusively in the contemplation of God and in communion with Him, is the way to grow in the spirit of Mortification, without which spirit the bare acts of it have little or no value.

CHAPTER XX.

LOVE FOR THE BRETHREN A TEST OF OUR LOVE FOR GOD.

"*If a man say, I love God, and hateth his brother, he is a liar: for he that loveth not his brother whom he hath seen, how can he love God whom he hath not seen?*"—1 JOHN iv. 20.

IT was remarked, at the opening of the last Chapter, that the Holy Scriptures, which aim everywhere at the inculcation of principles rather than of sentiments, furnish practical tests for ascertaining how far we are under the influence of the love of God. One of these practical tests was considered in that Chapter. We saw that Mortification was the negative side of the love of God—that in proportion as a man really embraces "the things which are above" with true affection, in that proportion will he "mortify his members which are upon the earth."

A second practical test is furnished to us, in the passage at the head of this Chapter, by the Apostle of love himself. Any pretence to the love of God, in the absence of the love of our neighbor, is a delusion,; what we think to be the love of God is in that case a mere sentiment, playing upon the surface of the soul, not a deeply-rooted principle which has the mastery of the will. And for this reason: God is an object of faith. His very existence is not made known to us by our senses. We have to "believe that He is." Our brother, on the other hand, is an object of sight. We come across him; we have dealings with him; we need not to make any effort of the mind to apprehend him; for his existence, his qualities, his character, force themselves upon our attention every moment, as he walks side by side with us along the path of life. Now, it is, of course, easier to walk by sight than by faith. And therefore it must be easier, much easier, to realize our neighbor's existence than to realize the existence of God. And, unless we thoroughly realize God's existence, it is out of the question that we can love Him.

Now, just pause here to consider the bearing of what has been said. At first sight, and before we weigh the meaning of the terms we employ, it might seem to be easier to love God than our neighbor. For the idea of God, which we form (and which we ought to form) in our minds, embraces every perfection, and excludes every imperfection. We think of Him, and we are right in thinking of Him, as not only infinitely powerful and wise, but as infinitely loving, gracious, bountiful, truthful, just, and holy. Our neighbor, on the other hand, like ourselves, is compassed about with infirmities, infirmities with which we come day by day into rude (and sometimes hostile) collision, infirmities forced upon us by the fact that we see him, and (if I may say so) feel him. He has hard angles, and we run up against them; awkward tempers, irritating eccentricities, ways which thwart our ways; he is vain and conceited, or he is cold and reserved, or he is ungracious, or even sometimes rude. And it often happens (which is very perverse in him) that the side which he turns to society is his unlovable side; he has much good in him which he never shows, and which nobody would believe to exist, were it not that character will in the long-run transpire to those around us, do what we will to throw a veil over it. Now, this being the case with some, possibly with many, in whose company we have to travel along the path of life, we might be disposed to say, on being told that the love of our neighbor is much easier than the love of God: "How can this be? A considerable degree of forbearance is necessary in order to love my neighbor at all; but in God all is lovely, all is gracious, all is beautiful, all is attractive to the heart; God has no unamiable side; God (and Christ who is His Image) is the infinite Amiability, and draws His children to His Bosom with those allurements which are naturally engaging to the human heart, 'with cords of a man, with bands of love.'"

How shall we maintain the Apostle's position against an objection of this kind? The answer is plain and very instructive. It is easier to have a certain sentimental drawing toward an idea of God, than to love our brother. But then *to have a sentimental drawing toward an idea of God, is not to love God.* It is easy to construct in the mind a pretty imagination, and to feel charmed and fascinated by it; but this, if we go not beyond this, is loving an abstraction, not loving a person. Before loving a person, we must really and truly apprehend his existence; and, in the case of a person whom we have not seen and cannot see, this true and realizing apprehension can only come from faith. Imagination is not faith, but only the natural faculty in man's heart which corresponds to faith. To imagine God is not to believe in Him. Anybody can imagine God by a mere exercise of his natural powers. But no man can have faith in God as a living Person, on whom all things are momentarily dependent, but by the supernatural power of Grace. To grasp the Personality of God, to apprehend Him, not as a law, nor as an influence, but as an actually existent, conscious Being, who stands in certain close relations to us, and has dealings with us every moment, and so to apprehend this truth as to be brought under its power—this, so far from being easy, is an arduous achievement. Whereas our brother's existence and character are obvious to the senses; there is *no* difficulty in realizing *that*. With God there are two processes to be gone through, the apprehending Him first, and then the loving Him. In our neighbor's case we have no more to do than to love him. The apprehension of *him* comes in the course of nature, and as a matter of experience.

The love of our neighbor would require for its full and adequate discussion a separate treatise. In the present Chapter we can only consider its profound connection with the love of God (which will serve to fence off certain errors connected with the subject), and the practical tests to which any profession of this love must be brought.

I. A word, first, on the intimate connection subsisting between the love of God and that of our neighbor. The second is wrapped up in the first, and for this reason: What we are required to love in our neighbor is the image of God in him. Every soul has a fragment of this image in its lowest depth, though it may be overlaid by all manner of rubbish—infirmity, imperfection, frivolity, sin. There is some one point in which every soul is accessible to compassion and sympathy, or to an exhibition of truth which condemns it—some one echo, in short, which it is adapted to make to some one chord of truth and love—some one spark (if it have not been quenched by persistence in wilful sin) of chivalrous, generous, heroic feeling. Just as in every mind also there is a capacity—not, it may be, for the usual class of acquirements, nor for those which yield a return in the way of honor and emolument, but—for something. Every human intelligence can construct something or imagine something; it has a power of development in a certain direction, or it would not be a human intelligence, but merely the instinct of an animal. And as the skilful portrait-painter studies to bring out upon his canvas, not the literal resemblance of the features, as they appear in the wear and tear of daily life, but the characteristic expression (or soul), caught only once or twice in happy moments, and even then requiring an effort of the imagination to extricate it from the gross lineaments of flesh and blood, so the true Christian studies the happy art of making the most of every one with whom he is thrown in contact—of recognizing in each soul, and of eliciting from it (to recognize is the way to elicit), that feature of heart and mind in which stands the relationship of that particular soul to God. It is this character of the man, disentangled from the infirmities and imperfections which, in consequence of the Fall, have gathered over and concealed it—it is, in short, *the true self of our neighbor*—that we are required to love.

And this observation places our duty in a clearer light. We are not required to love infirmities or imperfections; nay, we could not do so, if required; for infirmities and imperfections are naturally repelling. Our brother's true self is the object upon which our love is to fasten; and as to his infirmities and imperfections, which he shares with us in virtue of our common deterioration by the Fall, those are to be borne with and overlooked out of regard to his true self, and to the filial relation which this true self bears to God.—Does this distinction between a man's true self and his failings seem to any of my readers subtle and overstrained? Let me say that, under another view of the subject, it is universally accepted. What is the meaning of saying (as we often do) that God loves the sinner, while He hates the sin? Nothing can be truer. I need not say that God not only does, but *must*, hate sin in its every form; that between Him and insincerity, untruthfulness, peevishness, petulance, ill-temper—above all, perhaps, between Him and selfishness—there must be an eternal antipathy. And yet nothing is more certain than that, while God hates my selfishness and untruthfulness, He deeply and tenderly loves *me* with an individualizing love. I say an individualizing love; for is it not written that Christ "by the grace of God tasted death for EVERY MAN"—not for the human race generally, nor (I may say) for the human race at all, except as made up of individual souls (Christ did not die for abstractions, but for persons!), but for each individual of the race singly and separately, as much as if there had been no other person in the world to die for? And as for my sins and infirmities, these (blessed be His Name!) are no hinderance to His love: He loves me through them all (even the worst of them), that He may love me out of them, if I will only let Him. Day after day He bears with them, though they are eradicated very slowly, manifesting infinite patience toward me, because He is conscious of an infinite strength. Now, He would have me love my neighbor exactly as He loves me, fastening my regard upon his true self, upon the feature of God's image which is reflected in his soul, and bearing with his infirmities out of this esteem for the true self. Must it not be practicable? It is what He is constantly doing to me.

II. But it is with the love of our neighbor exactly as it is with the love of God; the pressing it only in an abstract form may lead to sad delusion. Nothing is easier than, when we ourselves are in prosperity, to feel an expansion of the heart toward others, and a dim desire to shed happiness around us, and to mistake this for the charity which the Gospel requires from us. And therefore our love of our neighbor, no less than our love of God, must be brought to practical tests.

1. First: are we doing any thing to help our neighbor? making sacrifices for him, of money, or time, or pleasures? The Apostles John and James the Less seem both to be inspired with a holy jealousy of mere professions of benevolence. The first goes so far as to say that the profession is better away; he does not care for the blossom on the tree; let him see the fruits: "Hereby perceive we the love of God, be-

cause He laid down His life for us: and we ought to lay down our lives for the brethren." (Oh, the arduous standard of these Gospel precepts—if our brethren could be benefited by the sacrifice of our lives, if we felt that by submitting to death we should light among men a candle of truth, which should never be put out, we must not shrink even from that sacrifice!) "But whoso hath this world's good" (this world's life[1] or maintenance), "and seeth his brother have need, and shutteth up his bowels of compassion from him, how dwelleth the love of God"—not love FOR God, but God's love, or Christ's love, the love which He showed by sacrificing Himself for sinners—"in him? My little children, *let us not love in word, neither in tongue;* but in deed and in truth." And St. James to the same effect, though less strongly: "If a brother or sister be naked, and destitute of daily food, and one of you say unto them, Depart in peace; be ye warmed and filled; notwithstanding ye give them not those things which are needful to the body; what doth it profit?" Thus warned by God's Word, let us eschew all *professions* of benevolent sentiment, as connected with self-deception. And when such sentiments visit our hearts, let us set ourselves at once to do something of a practical kind for the succor and relief of our brethren. I say, *at once.* It is wonderful how soon impressions of this kind evaporate. Hearers, who happen to have little or nothing in their purses, will retire from a powerful charity sermon with their minds all in a glow of desire to assist the object advocated. But they do not strike while the iron is hot; and they find the glow has gone off when they

[1] Ὃς δ' ἂν ἔχῃ τὸν βίον τοῦ κόσμου, etc., etc., 1 John iii. 17.

wake on Monday. It is an excellent spiritual precept, whenever a good desire springs up in our heart, to stereotype and make it permanent—in other words, to bring the good desire to good effect by an effort in that direction. By such an effort the good desire, instead of vanishing like a writing on the sand, and leaving no trace behind it, passes into the character (much as digested food passes into the bodily frame), and contributes toward the formation and the force of it.

2. Then, secondly, our prayers for others furnish a good practical test as to the genuineness of the love we bear them. What approach are we making to the great model of the Lord's Prayer, which does not contain any petition exclusively directed to our own wants? Do we pray for others at all? And if we do, is this exercise considered by us merely as an ornamental appendage to our other prayers, but as in no wise essential to their acceptability with God? This is the view which hundreds of orthodox and estimable Christians secretly take of Intercessory Prayer. We have done enough, they think, if we have brought our own wants and sorrows under God's notice; but it is correct, and in ordinary cases desirable, to add a sentence or two invoking His blessing upon others. But surely this is not the standard set up by the Holy Scriptures on this subject. In the first place, as I have already said, there is the great Divine Model of Prayer, which seems to exclude all prayer for ourselves *alone*, being so constructed as to make it impossible for us to pray for ourselves, without at the same time praying for our brethren. And then there is the ground in reason for this construction of

the Model Prayer. When Our Blessed Lord would teach His disciples how words of prayer should become words of power, and take effect in the spiritual world, instead of falling paralyzed and impotent to the ground, He dwelt upon two, and only two, great points—they must be offered in faith: ("Therefore I say unto you, What things soever ye desire when ye pray, believe that ye receive them, and ye shall have them;") and they must be offered in love: ("And when ye stand praying, forgive, if ye have aught against any; that your Father also which is in heaven may forgive you your trespasses.") In other words, the offerer must recognize, while offering them, both his filial relationship to the Father of spirits, and his fraternal relationship to other spirits proceeding from the same Father. In the phenomena of Mesmerism (I am offering no opinion whatever upon their genuineness, but merely referring to them for an illustration), it is said that there must be some secret affinity between the operator and the subject, if the effect is to be produced. The motion of the hands will, in the absence of this affinity, be a mere beating of the air without any visible result. In like manner, the uplifted hands of prayer will not draw down an influence from above—its words, and even cries, will be spoken into the air—unless first we bring our minds into affinity with the Infinite Mind of God. And this it is impossible to do, first, without faith: ("He that cometh to God *must believe* that He is, and that He is a rewarder of them that diligently seek Him;") and, secondly, without love. For God's Nature is Love—Love to all created spirits—and he must necessarily repel those who come to Him in a spirit not

His own. And therefore, in building up the structure of His own perfect prayer, Our Lord puts a word of faith first, and a word of love next: "Father of us" (such is the order of the words in the original); "Father," expressive of our relationship to Him; "of us," expressive of our relationship to the brethren. And he (and only he) who realizes these relationships, while he prays, shall pray with power, entering, as it were, into secret affinity with God, and touching the chords of God's heart.

Let me suggest, in conclusion, one method of realizing the latter of these relationships, which may, under God's blessing, prove effectual. Seek to make your prayers for others specific, as far as your knowledge of their character and circumstances allows. Bring before your mind their trials and their needs, and endeavor to place yourself in their point of view, from which point you may be sure the trials and needs will look very different than they do from yours. Remember that to pray for them, without some measure of sympathy with them, would be a mere formality—the body of intercession without its animating soul. Pray for this sympathy, while you endeavor, by careful consideration of their case, to excite it within yourself: "Look not every man on his own things, but every man also on the things of others." Then offer for them the petitions which, if the case were yours, you would offer for yourself. And if the prayer seem as regards them to be ineffectual, yet it shall be accepted on your own behalf as an act of love. The dove which Noah sent forth, when she could find no resting-place outside the ark, came back again fluttering to the window. And similarly our efforts for others, whether of prayer or benevolence, are not lost. If *they* are not benefited by them, *we* are: in increase of light, and power, and comfort, in whispers of mercy and peace, they return again into our bosom.

CHAPTER XXI.

THE LOVE OF GOD A PRINCIPLE RATHER THAN A SENTIMENT.

"*If ye love Me, keep My commandments.*"—JOHN xiv. 15.

THE last discourses of Our Lord with His disciples, from which these words are taken, are full of pathos. The world is shut out; the Everlasting Father and His little children are taking their last farewells one of the other in absolute privacy; the only unfaithful one of the twelve has taken his leave of the supper-room, and gone out upon the execution of his dark design; Our Lord is sure of the sincerity of those who remain, and accordingly He pours out His heart toward them in accents of most touching tenderness. But yet there is a certain element in His conversation, which makes us observe that, while there is pathos in the interview, there is no sentiment (perhaps I should rather say, no sentimentality) in it. Sentiment is an emotion of the heart indulged for its own sake, because the indulgence is pleasurable at the moment, and will be pleasurable in the retrospect; but there is nothing of this kind in the last interview of Christ with His chosen ones. There is here no luxury of grief indulged for a moment, that it may be looked back upon afterward with a melancholy satisfaction; the pathos flows out of the position, and out of the deep earnestness of the work done in the position. The Good Shepherd, about to leave His little flock, addresses Himself to impress upon their memory those particular topics of consolation, encouragement, and warning, of which He knew they would have most need in His absence. And He strikes in their ears from time to time a certain note, which reminds them that He will repudiate a mere sentimental attachment. He tells them again, in these last moments, what He had told them more publicly in the Sermon on the Mount, that no affection will He acknowledge, but such as takes the practical form of obedience; that the love which He expects from them is a principle, not a sentiment; that it lies in the will and moral choice, rather than in the emotions. Thus in the passage at the head of the chapter: "If ye love Me, keep My commandments." And again in ver. 21, "He that hath My commandments, and keepeth them, he it is that loveth Me." And again in ver. 23, "If a man love Me, he will keep My words." And again, in chap. xv., "If ye keep My commandments, ye shall abide in My love." And again, "Ye are My friends, if ye do whatsoever I command you." These are only reiterations to the innermost circle of the disciples of the more public warnings given earlier in His Ministry: "Not every one that saith unto Me, Lord, Lord, shall enter into the kingdom of heaven; but he that doeth the will of My Father which is in heaven;" and again: "My mother and My brethren are these which hear the word of God, and do it."

We have touched frequently, in these closing Chapters, upon the difference between sentiment and principle; and it appears to me desirable, by way of impressing what has been said, that this point should be argumentatively discussed and thoroughly explored; for it has more than an incidental importance. The distinction between the emotions and the affections—between sentiments and principles—is one which it would be of infinite service to true religion to make clear. *First, it would serve for the detection of hypocrisy.* There are many persons (many in the ranks of the Church, though perhaps more among the sects) who mistake lively emotions of compunction, remorse, joy, triumph, for the graces of the Gospel, repentance, faith, love, and humble assurance. A life of ecstatic feeling, crowned by a sort of rapture in death, is their great idea of saintliness. They have never sufficiently weighed the truth that the hearers who receive the word with joy, and in whose hearts it springs up with the rapidity and luxuriance of a tropical plant, are not the right sort of hearers; their hearts want depth and moisture, and so they dure but for awhile, and in time of temptation fall away.—Again, the distinction we are going in quest of will serve, when found, *to console many a down-hearted Christian.* There are many who, partly from constitutional causes, partly from the natural temperament of their minds, partly from their having approached Religion rather from the side of duty than from that of privilege, have by no means that flow of feeling connected with the subject which they desire to find in themselves. They pray earnestly for a contrite heart, but feel very little sensible grief for their sins. They look hard, as they have been advised to do, at the details of our Saviour's

Passion; but they feel no sympathy with the Divine Sufferer. They embrace God's promises, as far as their intention is concerned; but without unction, fervor, or sensible delight. They embrace God's will, when it prescribes either duty or suffering, but without those warm emotions of gratitude and confidence, of which they could desire to be conscious. They have been instructed (and most rightly instructed) that the surrender of the heart is what God requires first and before all things else, and that true Religion stands in certain tempers or affections of the soul, which flow out of faith—even in "love, joy, peace, long-suffering, gentleness, goodness, fidelity,[1] meekness, temperance." They cannot perceive by sensible emotions the presence of these fruits of the Spirit within them; and therefore they altogether question their presence. And sometimes, when the animal spirits are low, either from failure of health, or from some shock received in the order of God's Providence, the distress resulting from the dryness and hardness of their own minds amounts almost to dismay.

Now by way of establishing the fact of there being

[1] I translate thus πίστις in Gal. v. 22, because I hardly think that it can here mean the *fundamental* grace of the Christian character, out of which all others are developed. Bengel, if I remember rightly (I am quoting him from memory), interprets similarly. His observation is to this general effect: that love and joy are graces exercised *toward God;* peace, a grace exercised *reciprocally between neighbors* ("Have peace *one with another*"); long-suffering, gentleness, goodness, faith, meekness, graces exercised *toward our neighbor;* temperance, a grace exercised *toward ourselves.* Faith, therefore, is here that quality in another man, which makes one feel that one can depend upon him—trustworthiness.

a difference between the affections and the emotions (and thus clearing the way to see what this difference is), we may point to ordinary life as furnishing abundant scope for the one, with but little scope for the other. Take the life of nine-tenths of the community in a civilized country. The ordinary relationships are contracted; the ordinary pursuits are engaged in; the ordinary recreations are resorted to as a relief; the ordinary, and not more than the ordinary, casualties occur; there may be troubles, but they are hardly calamities; there may be gratifications, but they do not deserve the name of great successes. Life under such circumstances moves mechanically in the groove of routine, and is seldom so disturbed as to be altogether thrown out of the groove. In such a life, because there is in it little or no incident or reverse, there is but little play for the emotions. Feelings are seldom strongly excited, because there is nothing to excite them. The soul is never harrowed with fear; for what is there in modern civilized life, with all the securities offered by it for the person and property, to arouse fear? And as for any of those bright hopes, which were the sun-gleams of the soul in early youth, they are fast dying out, and every additional year decks the future, not with rainbow colors, but with a soberer gray; and the love of friends and relations, however much its power is silently felt, is singularly undemonstrative. Yet who shall say, because of this dearth of emotion, that, in the heart of the large majority of men who live this regular and civilized life, the affections are dead? It is simply untrue to say so. If you placed these same men and women amidst incidents, surprises, and reverses, such as are portrayed in tragedies or romances, the emotions of fear, hope, indignation, love, would show themselves, at the various crises furnished by such a life, with a vigor which would reveal a force of character you little suspected. Something of this kind is often seen, when war breaks out, and many men, who have been hitherto the frivolous members of a frivolous society, being placed in positions of trust or danger, surprise the world by their chivalry or their gallant endurance of hardships. They had fortitude and generous sentiments in their hearts at home; but at home the occasion for their display was lacking. And so with the domestic affections, which bind us together; they run still and deep (the stiller oftentimes the deeper), and *only make a noise* (or, in other words, only show themselves in emotion) *when a crisis occurs.* When our friends are taken from us by death we shed tears, and feel that a blight has come over our life; but while they are by our sides, we acquiesce in the consciousness of their sympathy, without any rapturous expressions of our feeling for them. Perhaps the only demonstrations of affection made in the course of ordinary life are an unreserved confidence, and a desire to please in little things. The affection for our friends is the same, while they are by our sides, as when they are taken away: but it does not pass into emotion, except when we have actually lost, or are in imminent danger of losing, them.

What has been said holds good of the affections in their application to Religion; for here too they are governed by the same laws as in the natural life of man. In the spiritual as in the natural man, lively emotion and deep affection are different things, and the absence of the latter can be never safely inferred from the nonappearance of the former. All the sudden crises and abrupt transitions of the spiritual life will no doubt be attended with emotion. All conversions which are more or less sudden in their character (I use this language advisedly, intending to intimate that conversion *may be* sudden in certain cases, but is no less genuine when achieved very gradually), all plunges of the soul from the darkness of ignorance and levity into the light of Divine Truth and religious privilege, must necessarily involve liveliness of feeling. The fear of Hell will sometimes shake the soul to its centre, and possess it with an earnest horror, altogether new to it. A sense of the Saviour's exceeding great Love will pour itself like a warm beam of the sun into every cranny of the consciousness, and the sensation will be full of delight. And he who has thus tasted that the Lord is gracious will be minded as St. Peter was at the Transfiguration. Ecstasy of feeling is attractive to all of us; it varies the monotony of existence; it lifts the mind easily and without effort into a frame which the moral sense cannot but approve; it is a welcome relief from the wear and tear, the drudgery and responsibility, of little homely duties. So we plead that it may endure—that we may be allowed to build a tabernacle upon the mount, where the Lord appears to us in glory, and the voice from heaven falls upon our ear. This is the real meaning of all who aim at what are called revivals in the Church. What they really seek, and what they will not be contented without seeing, is not so much the deep silent work of grace, by which men are brought to give up their hearts to the Lord, as the quickening of surface emotions on the subject of Religion, the stretching the soul on the rack of fear and anxiety, and then its inundation with all the reliefs and refreshments of Grace. They would fain galvanize the soul into life by a sudden shock; and sometimes they confound the galvanic action, which at most can only be the cause, with the life, which is the effect. But the true life of the soul is in its affections, not in its emotions. *Emotions are impossible* (according to the law of our minds), *except at a crisis and moment of convulsion.* And he who seeks for them under ordinary circumstances will run the risk of making his religion morbid. There are two safe signs, in our normal spiritual life, that we love Christ—the same which indicate the reality of our love to those around us. One is *confidence*—a compliance with that invitation of the Psalmist: "Trust in Him at all times, ye people; pour out your hearts before Him; for God is our hope." The habit of exposing the contents of the heart to Christ, of referring all our actions to His will, of commending all our troubles to His care, and all our difficulties to His direction, the realizing Him (not perhaps as much as we could wish to do, but in some measure) as being by our side, always sympathizing, always inviting our confidence, always ready and willing to help us, the being sincere in all our dealings with Him, and perfectly single-minded in seeking to know His will—this is one great test of love for Him, which, if really found in us in a small degree, is worth a large amount of high-flown feeling.—And the second test is, that we seek to please Him. A simple test enough, as it would seem on hearing the first statement of it, but yet involving more than we might at first sight imagine. For an effort to please Christ involves a sense of Christ's living Personality. We do not talk of pleasing a law, but simply of satisfying its requirements. We do not talk of pleasing an influence, but simply of acting in conformity with it. The attempt to please a person involves a recognition that he stands to us in a certain relationship, has certain thoughts about us, is liable to be affected by our conduct, is susceptible of emotions from our way of acting. To attempt to please Christ is not only to act in compliance with the general indications of His will which are made to us in His Word, but to be on the watch for opportunities of doing Him service, and to embrace those opportunities whenever they arise; it is to be guided by His Eye, as well as by the express directions of His Voice, and to find in the sense of His favor and approving smile the strongest stimulus to duty. Whoever feels and acts thus toward Him *must* love Him, *however little of sensible emotion he may experience.* The love of friends in daily life is shown by unreserved confidences, and by a study to please in trifles; and it is the greatest of all mistakes to suppose that, where these confidences pass, and these endeavors are made, there is no affection, because there is no passionate flow of feeling, or, in other words, because there is no strong emotion. Emotion may be defined as *affection quickened by a crisis.* But then it is not at all essential to the existence or genuineness of an affection that it should be thus quickened. Take an illustration from the animal frame. Physical emotion may be defined as a quickening of the pulses by a sudden surprise, or danger, or deliverance. If a man falling over a precipice, and having a momentary apprehension of being dashed to pieces, lights on a grassy ledge only a few feet below him, and finds himself safe; or if a man in a dream, fancying he is about to be executed, wakes in the agonies of the crisis, and finds himself alive and in his own chamber, his heart begins to beat very fast; and this is physical emotion. But he may go on for days and months without any such experience, his heart beating and his blood circulating healthily and regularly, without his being conscious of it. Similarly with the mind. There may be a silent circulation of the affections in their usual channels, without that quick and morbid action of them which constitutes emotion.

Let us pause now to view one of the passages above quoted, in the light of these remarks, and see what aspect it assumes. "If ye love Me, keep My commandments;" that is, "In judging of your dispositions toward Me, I will not allow a mere emotion to pass current for love; love, or the love which I will recognize, is an affection, not an emotion; it is founded in the will or moral choice, and the will is the sphere in which it displays itself." This last position, "The will is the sphere in which all genuine love of Christ displays itself," is, in fact, the same truth which Our Lord here announces, thrown into a more abstract form. That we may go to the root of the subject, let us examine this statement, and seek to understand it thoroughly.

The love of Christ must show itself in the will; is, in fact, an affection of the will. The same may be said of all those holy tempers of the soul, which St.

Paul calls fruits of the Spirit; it is true of religious awe, of religious joy, of inward peace, of the charity which we should bear toward our fellow-men, of the hope of glory, that they are all affections of the will; they stand clear of the emotional and sensational part of the soul altogether; they belong to a higher part of our nature. Bear with me, dear reader, while I exhibit this briefly; the subject is not really difficult, though it may be a little abstract; and I believe sound views upon it to be all-important in the conduct of the spiritual life.

There are, then, in human nature *affections of the will*, which are quite distinct from, and sometimes show their distinctness by running contrary to, the emotions of the lower part of the mind. To show this more clearly, I will take the case of a virtuous heathen, animated (as we know many such heathens to have been) by a strong love of his country. Such a heathen had, of course, all the feelings to which mankind are ordinarily subject. He naturally loved his ease, shrunk from pain, feared wounds and death, loved the members of his family. But he had other loves and other fears, which urged him in a direction the very contrary of these lower motives. He hated tyranny, and could not bear to see his country oppressed by it; he loved liberty; he loved the happiness of his people; and this hatred and love were so strong, that he sacrificed to them ease, comfort, domestic happiness—nay, life itself. In doing so, he undoubtedly found a serene and high satisfaction, as every one who acts unselfishly is sure to do; but it was a satisfaction of the higher, and not the lower, instincts of our nature—of "the spirit," as the Apostle would have phrased it, not of "the soul."[1] His soul shrank from death, and feared it; but his spirit chose death, and carried the day. And he had his reward. Do not think he made such a sacrifice for nothing, or found nothing in the sacrifice. There is a high joy in self-abnegation for others, in disinterested enterprise, in a sense of duty gone through with in spite of difficulties. But this joy, you will at once perceive, is not that exuberance of animal spirits, that ebullition of the sensational nature, which often usurps the name, but a joy peculiar to the will, or moral faculty—a joy which conscience approves, and which, indeed, may be called the result of the smile of conscience on the soul. To cite the well-known words of South, in which he describes the passion of joy, as it existed before the Fall (a somewhat audacious speculation, by-the-way; what he is really describing is the joy of the *πνεῦμα*, or moral faculty, as distinct from the joy of the *ψυχή*, or sensational part—an affection of which we may all have experience): "Joy was not the mere crackling of thorns, the exultation of a tickled fancy, or a pleased appetite. Joy was

[1] The reference is to 1 Thes. v. 23, where "soul" and "spirit" are carefully distinguished; also to Heb. iv. 12, where their close union is implied. Also to 1 Cor. ii. 14; 1 Cor. xv. 44, 46; where "the man of the soul," "the body which is of the soul" (*ὁ ψυχικὸς, τὸ σῶμα ψυχικὸν*), is contradistinguished from "the man of the spirit"—"the body which is of the spirit" (*ὁ πνευματικὸς, τὸ σῶμα πνευματικόν*). Also observe how in St. Jude (v. 19), those who are characterized as *ψυχικοὶ* ("men of the soul"), are said "not to have the Spirit"—meaning, doubtless, the Holy Spirit; but the phraseology seems to intimate that the ideas presented to the writer's mind by the words *ψυχή* and *πνεῦμα* were more or less incompatible.

then a masculine and a severe thing; the recreation of the judgment, the jubilee of reason. It commenced upon the solidities of truth, and the substance of fruition. It did not run out in voice or indecent eruptions, but filled the soul, as God does the universe, silently, and without noise."

Now, the remark which holds good of joy holds good also of love, and of all the other affections. There is a love of the soul, or emotional part of our nature; and there is a love of the spirit, or the will, or the moral faculty. In ordinary parlance, the merest fancy for another person—a fancy able to give no account of itself, and therefore confessedly a whim—a fancy light as air, which has not the ballast of a single grain of esteem, commonly usurps the sacred name of love, and passes current for that affection. There is nothing of the judgment in it; and often it would not stand the test of the least self-denial for the sake of its object, if that test were applied. "Now," says Our Blessed Saviour in the passage we are commenting upon, "this is not the kind of love which I require, or which I can be satisfied with. Your love for Me must be an affection of the will; it must be a moral choice of Me, in preference to sin and the world; and must show itself in embracing My will, both by active obedience and passive submission. It must be grounded upon a perception of My excellence, and of the benefits received from Me, and must enable you to find in the single-minded effort to please Me a satisfaction purer, higher, and of a different order, than is to be found in any earthly gratifications."

It is quite conceivable that the first disciples of Christ may have needed this warning, even more than we ourselves. "Though we have known Christ after the flesh" (says St. Paul, identifying himself for the moment with the original Apostles, and throwing himself into their position), "yet now henceforth know we Him no more." Quite natural must it have been for St. Peter and St. John to know Christ "after the flesh," and to love Him after the flesh. The winning suavity of His demeanor; His condescending gentleness to the weak, the fallen, the suffering, mingled with His heroic defiance of hypocrisy, and His stern love of Truth; His patient submissiveness to the Father's will; and the entrancing radiations of the Godhead, which must have sometimes struggled forth from His voice, features, and gestures—must, one would think, have surrounded Him in their minds with (what I must call) a sentimental beauty, and must have conciliated to Him a sentimental affection. But He here makes known to them that this affection would not suffice. Their love was not to be manifested by tender regrets, fond lingering on the old bygone days when He companied with them in the flesh, fond associations of places connected with Him, fond reminiscences of His manner and words. They were to know Him and to love Him "after the spirit"—not as their human friend, but as their ever-present God, "the strength of their heart and their portion forever." He gave them, indeed, a precious token in the Eucharist, by which to call to mind His sojourn with them; but this single condescension to the love of sentiment He crowned with the dignity of a Sacrament, and made it for His Church generally not so much the means of commemorating an absent, as of communicating with a present Saviour. And in my judgment, it is a great evidence of the inspiration which held the minds of the Apostles in check, while they wrote, that the mere love of sentiment toward Christ is never heard in their writings; St. Peter and St. John may be mentioned historically in the Gospels as manifesting feeling of this kind on one or two occasions; but in their Epistles you find no trace of such love; the human friend seems to have vanished from their memory; and Jesus, viewed under the light of Pentecost, is simply the Redeeming God, the One Mediator, the only Name given among men whereby we must be saved.

Reader, are you looking at Him in the point of view in which they present Him? Is your love for the Saviour something more and deeper than a mere sentimental appreciation of the beauty of His character? How far does it reside in the will—this love? how far in the judgment and moral sense? I am sure that there may be, even in ourselves, a picturesqueness of impression about Christ without the least real appreciation of Him. Do you live much with Him, and love to live with Him, in thought and in prayer? Do you honor Him by drawing Him into use in all His offices of Grace? Can you yield up your will into His hands, to choose for yourself nothing else than He chooses for you? Does the satisfaction of trying to please Him—an effort which is never made in vain—excel every other in a certain high and pure flavor? These are the questions which must determine the genuineness of our love for Him. And genuine love is the only safe evidence of genuine faith in Him. And on faith in Him is suspended our salvation. On them only who love Cri s t rests the

Apostolic benediction: "Grace be with all them that love our Lord Jesus Christ in sincerity." And, lest any suppose that, though the love of Him be laudable, indifference to Him is excusable, the same Apostle sounds in our ears the extremest malediction on those who love Him not: "If any man love not the Lord Jesus Christ, let him be Anathema Maranatha."

CHAPTER XXII.

WHAT SHUTS OUT CHRIST FROM OUR HEARTS?

"*There was no room for them in the inn.*"—LUKE ii. 7.

THOSE who have followed along our course of argument in the present treatise will probably come to the conclusion, that, if Holiness be what we have described it to be, the great majority of persons who pass for religious with themselves and others, nay, to whom the credit of being in a greater or less degree religious cannot be denied, are very backward in the pursuit of it. It may be profitable in this concluding Chapter to explore the causes of this backwardness. In doing so we shall see how to remedy what is amiss in us. And this accidental advantage also will accrue, that we shall be furnished with tests of spiritual progress, which we may apply to our own hearts.

Now, first, it is evident that our backwardness in true religion (or, in other words, in the knowledge and love of God) cannot in any measure be attributed to God Himself. God is a full-charged fountain of grace, who seeks to inundate every human intelligence and every human heart with His knowledge and His love. And we are told emphatically that He "is no respecter of persons;" He is not partial in the gifts and influences which He distributes. Human parents have often favorites among their children, whom they indulge with the coat of many colors, and the Benjamin's mess. But God has no such weak fondness in the treatment of ***His*** children; if He loves one better than another, it is because that one is worthier of His love. God in grace is like the sun in Nature, whose property it is to diffuse itself into every cranny, where it is not absolutely shut out; or like the precious dew of heaven, which drops indifferently on the salt places of the wilderness and on the rich and fruitful soil. God may say to His people, as the Apostle said to the Corinthians: "O my people, my mouth is opened unto you, my heart is enlarged. Ye are not straitened in me, but ye are straitened in your own bowels." These (though they are not so applied by the inspired writer) are exactly the accents in which God addresses every human soul. He is impatient of being perfectly loved by every soul; longing and desirous to pour out upon every soul the riches of His mercy and grace. He laments our narrowness; He beseeches us to be enlarged in our own hearts, and to make a worthy response to His affection.

And this reference leads us on a step further in our argument. It is in ourselves that we are straitened, and not in God. The sun may shed his light and warmth around, so that there is nothing hid from the heat thereof; but if a man constructs a hovel of boards, and stops the chinks between the boards with thick clay, the sun's rays cannot reach him. The dew may drop on the wilderness; but the salt places and the heath have no capacity of bringing forth a crop. The water of the river may be free to all comers, but without a vessel to contain it, it cannot be drunk, and with only a small vessel it cannot be drunk in large measure. Christ may come to the door of the inn, desiring to take up His abode there; but if there is no room for Him, He must be cradled in the manger outside. An inn—what an appropriate figure of the soul of man as it is by nature! What a multiplicity and what a prodigious variety of thoughts are always coming and going in the soul—the passengers these which throng the inn, and some of whom are so fugitive, that they do not even take up their abode there for the night! And what distraction, discomposure, and noise, do these outgoing and incoming thoughts produce, so that perhaps scarcely ever in the day is our mind collected and calm, except just for the few moments spent in private prayer before we lie down and when we rise—the hurry and confusion this, produced by the constant arrivals at, and departures from, an inn! And then some of these thoughts leave traces of defilement upon the soul, as they pass away, much as the careless and slovenly wayfarer leaves a soil or a rent upon the furniture. And, by way of completing the figure, Christ offers Himself at the door of the soul, as the passenger offers himself at the door of an inn. He seeks and longs to pass into the soul, that He may take up His abode there, and dwell in the heart by faith. "Behold," cries He, "I stand at the door, and knock: if any man hear My voice, and open the door, I will come in to him, and will sup with him, and he with Me." Oh! it is because we do not give Him *room* to work within us, that He works so faintly and feebly in our souls. It is because we bring such poor narrow hearts to Him, that we receive so little of His fulness. It is because we close ourselves up in the chamber of our selfishness, that we inhale so seldom the free, fresh atmosphere of His Spirit.

"There was no room for them in the inn." Now in what does the obstacle to Christ's entrance into our hearts consist? What is it which occupies the room which he seeks and condescendingly asks to occupy? Two things principally, under which all others will fall: first self-will, and then confidence in the creature for happiness.

1. First, self-will. The least trace of self-will excludes *pro tanto* God and His working from the soul. Absolute surrender to His Will and Word in every thing is the only condition on which the Lord will take up His abode in the depth of the soul, and give to the heart that calm and repose, which only His Presence can give. There are many Christians who, in seeking counsel and help from God, are not perfectly sincere, do not absolutely resign their will into His hand. They "keep back part of the price" in their dealings with Him, make reserves, and except certain districts of their life from His jurisdiction. They make the vain attempt to serve two masters, seeking to please God much, and themselves a little, in what they do. They are quite willing to pray, and read the Holy Scriptures, and attend Public Worship, and receive Holy Communion; but they have a great dislike to be pressed upon such points as systematic almsgiving, fasting, restraint of the tongue, self-denial in recreations, and mortification of the will, although they have a growing conviction in their minds that God requires from

them some measure of these things. They have not that delicate sensibility to God's inspirations which He loves to find in a soul, and which, when He does find it, enables Him to do many mighty works therein. You know how delicately a wind-vane is poised on the top of a building, so that with the slightest breath of wind (hardly sufficient on a hot day to fan the cheek agreeably) it veers round at once. It is so in Nature; but alas! in the moral world there is many a will which does not sit loose upon its pivot, but is fixed in the quarter to which its natural inclinations point, and which moves not, therefore, when the breath of God's Spirit seeks to turn it. And observe that we are not now speaking so much of cases in which there is a positive and well-defined right and wrong, and where the right and wrong might be determined by the Ten Commandments, or the Nine Beatitudes, or some other outward law. The principles of all right conduct and of all right sentiment are no doubt laid down with perfect clearness in the Holy Scripture; but we need for the conduct of daily life something more than this—it is necessary that we should see the right application of these principles to the ever-new and unforeseen openings for moral conduct which are continually presented to us. And this cannot be done by any outward rule, written and printed on paper, however perfect. It can only be done by submission to the will to what is called "the law of the Spirit of Life in Christ Jesus," that is, by compliance with the instigations which on such occasions the Spirit of God makes in the heart of those who are sincerely and singly desirous of pleasing Him. "We do not cease to pray for you," says St. Paul, "and to desire that ye might be filled with the knowledge of His will in all wisdom and spiritual understanding." Is it to be supposed that the Colossians were ignorant of the *literal* rule of duty, as given in the Law and expounded by Christ? No; what the Apostle supplicated for them was their direction by God's Holy Spirit as to His Will in particular cases. And again: "This I pray, that your love may abound yet more and more in knowledge and in all judgment; that ye may approve things that are excellent; that ye may be sincere and without offence in the day of Christ." As a man increases in earnest love to Christ, a delicate tact grows up within him, a spiritual instinct, which teaches him (without any book) what he ought to say and do, and what he had better avoid on each particular occasion. True love, even human and earthly love, is full of sensibilities; every one is aware how a person, whom he loves and seeks to please, will take a thing; without being wrong or coarsely offensive, it would be simply out of taste to say or do such and such things before such a person; they would jar upon him. There is something of the same kind in Divine love, the true lover of Christ being made sensitive by the Holy Spirit as to the line of conduct which pleases or displeases Him. "I will instruct thee and teach thee in the way which thou shalt go;" this is God's gracious promise by the Psalmist: "and *I will guide thee with mine eye.* Be ye not as the horse, or as the mule, which have no understanding; whose mouth must be held in with bit and bridle." Everybody knows what the guidance of a mother's eye is, while the children are around her. She need not speak. A glance and the expression of her countenance convey her wishes sufficiently. She looks up in alarm, and her eye warns the little ones away from danger; they are industrious, and her eye betokens approval; or they are too frolicsome, and a look of displeasure checks them. God's children, too, know the meaning of His eye. They know, by the glance He gives them, what path He would have them pursue, and what avoid. He never leaves them without an interior indication of His will, if they have but one desire, that of pleasing Him. And why these indications are so rarely made is, that God sees people are not quite disposed to accept them, not prepared in all things to move in the direction indicated. *The soul must be empty of self-will, before God can work in it.* We fulfil the desires of the flesh and of the mind—that is, we live according to the inclinations of Nature (not necessarily coarse or vicious inclinations), and the thoughts which she prompts. And while this is the case, Christ is shut out. "There is no room for Him in the inn."

2. The second thing which takes up room in the soul that Christ ought to occupy, is confidence in the creature for happiness. When I speak of the creature, I do not intend any other source of enjoyment but such as in itself is innocent. I merely mean worldly and created good in any of its forms—money, and the comforts money will buy; the sympathies of relations and friends, which no money can buy; and, in short the whole circle of blessings (commonly so called), which yet are not communion with God, and the knowledge and enjoyment of His perfections. Who shall say (without very special grace, and an extraornary measure of Divine illumination) how far his affection is set upon the earthly blessings with which

his cup is crowned; how far he is seeking in them a satisfaction which they can never give; how far, if they were removed, he could still console himself in that communion with the Father of spirits, which alone *does* satisfy? It is but too easy to deceive ourselves in this matter, while the earthly blessings remain with us. A man who swims upon bladders is apt to conceive that he could easily dispense with the support, and still keep his head above the water; nor is it easy to ascertain what resources he has in himself for swimming, until the artificial support is withdrawn. Let me say that by way of making trial of his children, of ascertaining, or rather of certifying *to themselves* (for He must know, without being certified) how far they have their treasure in heaven, and set their affection on things above, God sometimes removes our earthly treasures, and withdraws one or more of the swimming bladders. He strikes perhaps with death's dart some friend or relation, who was dear to us as our own soul, and to whom our affections were beginning to cleave idolatrously. Be warned, all you who have earthly treasures, and are conscious of prizing them exceedingly, that God is *certain* to act thus with all those who are (at the ground of their hearts) His true children, *if He sees the affections of trust and love twining too closely around the creature.* In very faithfulness to us He must then tear them away, and cause a painful bleeding of the heart. The only way to keep our earthly treasures, on the assumption that we are God's true people, is, while we thankfully hold them of God, to mortify all undue attachment to them, and sternly to refuse to idolize them. But this by the way.—Our most merciful Father, in the discipline to which we have referred, seldom (if ever) strips us quite bare of earthly blessings, and, even when He is obliged to use the pruning-knife most sternly, always leaves some green spray of comfort and some blossom of hope. And with the blessing (or blessings) left some of the risks are left also—in the sad tendency of the human heart to cleave to what is seen, *there can be no blessing without a risk.* The risk is, that the heart, shut out from one avenue of earthly comfort, may, instead of growing wiser by this discipline, intrench itself in the comforts that remain, may build other tabernacles for its indwelling (as Peter was desirous of doing on the mount), which shall stand it in no better stead than the first. Oh, how long it is before a soul can perfectly unlearn trust in the creatures! Does it ever completely unlearn this trust, while life lasts, and while the body of sin and death clogs it? I suppose not. And this I know for certain, without any supposition, that God is very patient and gentle with us in this matter, never laying upon us more than He sees we can well bear, never removing a blessing without a good reason, viewing with indulgence our every effort to struggle into independence of His creatures, and always restoring comfort to the mourner after the object has been achieved. This is the lesson of the history of Job. Job was subjected to a most frightful ordeal. He was stripped bare of every thing which makes life (I do not say enjoyable, but) tolerable—property, esteem, health, relations. "Ye have heard of the patience of Job," says St. James, "and have seen the end of the Lord; that the Lord is very pitiful, and of tender mercy." Now, unless we take fully into account the indulgence shown by God to His children amidst their trials, and the graciousness with which He accepts their every effort to maintain, under such circumstances, a right frame of mind, we might be surprised at the Scripture's attributing *patience* to Job. He certainly bemoaned himself very grievously, wished he had never been born, requested for himself that he might die, and so on. But, under all his groaning, God saw the germ of a true resignation in those early words of his: "The Lord gave, and the Lord hath taken away; blessed be the name of the Lord" . . . "What? shall we receive good at the hand of God, and shall we not receive evil?" God, considering the excessive burdensomeness of Job's trials, and the dimness with which the compensatory life beyond the grave had been revealed before the Incarnation, accounted this true germ of patience for patience; and, when He had taught Job the spiritual lessons which he needed to learn, returned to him with a prosperity in every respect double of that which he had originally enjoyed.

But it may be pertinently asked whether all appreciation and enjoyment of created good (in any shape, however innocent) takes up the room in the heart which God ought to occupy—whether (to put the question in other words) all pleasures, except such as are of a religious character, are denied to a Christian? *Most assuredly not.* The attempt to crush in ourselves our appreciation of earthly blessings would, as unnatural, recoil upon us. And such an attempt would be as unscriptural as it is unnatural. Of the asceticism which in the latter days should lay its ban upon marriage and upon meats, and which should usurp in the minds of some the place of Christian mortification, St. Paul says[1] (what stronger thing could he say?) that it is a departure from the faith, a doctrine inculcated by devils and seducing spirits. And we may say of the whole compass of earthly blessings what there he says of food: "Every creature of God is good, and nothing to be refused, if it be received with thanksgiving." It is not mere enjoyment of the creature, *but trust in the creature to satisfy, all the deep cravings of the soul*, which excludes God and Christ from the heart. Nay; a moderate and chastened enjoyment of the creature actually contributes to our sanctification, inasmuch as it acts as a stimulant to gratitude. We must learn the art of tasting the various blessings with which God crowns our cup, without being engrossed or taken up with them, without suffering them to quench the high aspirations of our soul after Communion with God. This is a lesson which it takes long practice, much self-control, and great discipline of God's Providence, and Spirit, to teach. Hear the language of experience: "I have never leaned toward my comforts," says Mr. Cecil, "without finding them give way. A sharp warning has met me that these are aliens; and as an alien live thou among them. We may take up the pitcher *to drink*, but, the moment we begin *to admire*, God in love to us will dash it to pieces." Perhaps the quaint and yet graceful imagery of good George Herbert may assist us in understanding what is required of us in this matter:

"All creatures have their joy:
  Yet, if we rightly measure,
  Man's joy and pleasure
Rather hereafter than at present is.

[1] 1 Tim. iv. 1, 3, 4.

> Not that he may not here
> Taste of the cheer;
> But, as birds drink and straight lift up their head,
> So he must sip, and think
> Of better drink
> He may attain to after he is dead."

But, alas! men will not *sip;* for they find temperance very hard—much harder than total abstinence. They will either drink to intoxication, or not taste a drop. The one party are led by their lusts; the other are perverse in declining what Heaven gives as a sweet relief. Both are true children of mother Eve, who ate greedily the forbidden fruit; while at the same time she peevishly aggravated the Divine requirements. Whereas God had said only, "Ye shall not eat of the fruit," she added to His word a restriction out of her own naughty heart: "God hath said," she murmured, "ye shall not eat of it, *neither shall ye touch it,* lest ye die." The whole doctrine of asceticism, branded by St. Paul as a "doctrine of devils," is wrapped up in that clause, "neither shall ye touch it." Eve had admitted the insinuations of the seducing spirit, before she so misrepresented the precept of the Blessed God.

In conclusion: let every reader apply to himself what has been said, by asking whether the reason of his slow advance in grace may not be that, either by self-will, or by trust in creatures, he gives Christ no room to work in his heart. Are you heartily willing to be all, and to do all, that God requires? And doth your soul pant after Him, "as the hart desireth the water-brooks;" or, on the other hand, *would you be well contented with His blessings, in the absence of*

Himself? This earthly contentment will, *must* exclude Him from the soul. There is no room for Him in the inn, so long as there is no desire but for His gifts—none for Himself. In that case, repulsed from the door of the heart, which He has in vain wooed and sought to win, He must lie without, His head filled with dew, and His locks with the drops of the night. Good reader, pray that it may be neither your own case, nor that of him who now bids you ADIEU.

THE END.

BIBLE TEACHINGS IN NATURE.

By the Rev. HUGH MacMILLAN.

1 Vol., 12mo. Cloth. Price, $2.00.

From the N. Y. Observer.

"These are truly original and delightful discourses, in which investigations of natural science are skilfully and often eloquently employed to establish divine revelation, and to illustrate its truths."

From the Hartford Morning Post.

"This is a work of rare merit in its way, and may be read with great profit and interest by lovers of Nature—by those who have the gift of *insight*, and who can look up 'through Nature to Nature's God' and see the 'invisible power and Godhead in the things which He has made.'"

From the Eastern Argus.

"The healthy mind delights in the beauties and mysteries of Nature, and this volume will be found both instructive and interesting."

From the Daily Enquirer.

"This is a beautifully written work, intended to make the studies of the Bible and of Nature doubly attractive, by pointing out the harmony which exists between them as revealed to the earnest students of both."

From the Norfolk County Journal.

"The author sees God everywhere revealed in the development of Nature,—finds Him in the works of pure and unobtrusive beauty; in the grand and impressive in scenery, and in the wonderful manifestations with which the world abounds."

www.ingramcontent.com/pod-product-compliance
Lightning Source LLC
LaVergne TN
LVHW010217110826
845151LV00004B/1115

* 9 7 8 1 4 2 5 5 2 8 2 9 4 *